La Dolce Cucina

La Dolce Cucina

The Italian Dessert Cookbook

Anna Bruni Seldis

COLLIER BOOKS

A Division of Macmillan Publishing Co., Inc.

NEW YORK

COLLIER MACMILLAN PUBLISHERS

LONDON

Macmillan Publishing Co., Inc.
866 Third Avenue, New York, N.Y. 10022
Collier-Macmillan Canada Ltd.

Line drawings by Marilyn M. Grastorf.

Library of Congress Cataloging in Publication Data

Seldis, Anna Bruni.
   La dolce cucina.

   In English.
   1. Desserts.   2. Cookery, Italian.   I. Title.
II. Title: The Italian dessert cookbook.
[TX773.S37 1974b]   641.8'6   74-6263
ISBN 0-02-010300-X

La Dolce Cucina is published in a hardcover edition by Macmillan Publishing Co., Inc.

First Collier Books Edition 1974

Printed in the United States of America

Table of Contents

Nut Cakes and Cookies

Ices, Ice Creams, and Spumoni

Creams, Puddings, Mousses, and Souffles

Regional Specialties

Introduction
La Dolce Cucina

THE PURPOSE OF this book is to present to the English-speaking public a variety of Italian desserts from different parts of Italy. Most of these desserts have never been available in this country, and the recipes for them have never been translated. Yet unlike French and Danish pastry, Italian desserts do not require great amounts of butter, eggs, and sugar, and are, therefore, less fattening, less expensive, and more healthful than the sweets Americans are accustomed to eating.

Southern Italian desserts are best known in this country, having been publicized by generations of Italo-American women, for whom pastry making according to the old recipes was part of a traditional way of life that they maintained in the New World. However, there is hardly any mention of northern Italian desserts in the brief chapters on Italian pastry which appear in the English-language Italian cookbooks. This is a pity. Northern Italian desserts, like Austrian, Danish, and French ones, place an emphasis on the delicate blending of various ingredients which produces an effect of lightness and subtlety.

While popular and traditional Italian dishes, together with regional specialties, can be found in America in most Italian restaurants, the repertoire of desserts in these restaurants is usually very limited, consisting mainly of two- or three-layer cakes made either of some kind of light, spongy dough soaked in rum, or flaky pastry covered with custard or chocolate sauce. The regional specialties (with the exceptions of a few made commercially and sold in packages) and the other recipes I am including in this book are desserts which can usually be tasted only in Italian homes and which have been handed down from one generation to the other.

The making of desserts has been my favorite hobby since my early teens, and I have invented numerous recipes myself which are included here together with those I collected through the years. Being a Venetian, whose father and grandparents came from Abruzzi, my experience and knowledge of desserts cover a wide range which goes from the north to the south of Italy.

My mother, although a good cook, never indulged in making desserts, preferring to buy them in the excellent Venetian pastry shops. However, when she saw that I was interested in dessert-making, she let me try out a few recipes that I had obtained from relatives and friends and written down in my first notebook. Eventually I filled several notebooks with dessert recipes, my own and those of others. And finally I have come to write this book.

I have divided it into eight chapters. In the first I give the recipes for basic doughs—that is, the most common Italian doughs, which are the base for a variety of desserts. In the second I have recorded a number of cakes and pastries made with fruit; in the third cakes, cookies, and other desserts made with different kinds of nuts; and in the fourth five cakes in which neither flour nor fat is used. The fifth chapter is dedicated to fresh fruit desserts; the sixth to ices, ice cream, and spumoni; the seventh to creams, puddings, mousses, and soufflés; and the eighth to desserts that are strictly regional and not found everywhere in Italy.

To my knowledge this is the only cookbook dedicated entirely to Italian desserts; I hope it will provide prospective pastry makers and dessert cooks with a unique, useful, and enjoyable addition to their library.

Kitchen Utensils

DESSERT MAKING IS really a craft, and as in every other craft, special tools are required in order to work efficiently and to give the finished product the maximum of perfection in taste, texture, and also appearance—since the aesthetic element is an important part in the making of desserts.

You will need—

- *set of mixing bowls in different sizes (small, medium, and large)*
- *measuring spoons and cups*
- *set of wooden spoons*
- *large and small spatulas*
- *rubber scraper*
- *flour sifter*
- *paring knife*
- *apple corer*
- *food chopper*
- *small nut grinder—you can find it in most Italian grocery stores*
- *wire whip*
- *electric mixer or rotary egg beater*
- *3 sauce pans in different sizes*
- *frying pan*
- *molds—fluted, round, ring, and any other kind you may like*

- *double boiler*
- *2 muffin pans*
- *10" tube pan*
- *baking sheet*
- *8" and 9" pie pans—*
    8½ × 4½ × 3" pan—
    13 × 9 × 2" pan
- *spring pan*
- *individual custard cups*

- *wire cake racks*
- *wire strainer*
- *metal or plastic colander*
- *rolling board*
- *rolling pin*
- *cookie cutter and wheel*
    cutter
- *pastry brush*
- *serving dishes*

Optional—

- *decorating set for cakes and cookies (a paper cornucopia can be used instead)*
- *electric ice cream maker—this is not very expensive, and the difference in price between the electric and the manual is so small that unless you want to take it along on picnics, it is well worth paying a little more to get an electric one, which will save you a lot of time and work*

Basic Rules for
Dessert Making

THE FOLLOWING ARE a few simple rules to follow in order to make your dessert a success:

1. Read recipe through and assemble all ingredients and utensils. Follow directions carefully. You can experiment with variations of your own once you have acquired a certain expertise in pastry making.

2. Always sift flour before using; then add baking powder, if required, and sift again. When making cakes with raised dough, always add a pinch of salt, which enhances and blends flavors. Do not substitute wheat flour for pastry flour, since it is too heavy. All-purpose flour is not quite as fine, but it is all right, and I have used it in all of my recipes.

3. Beat egg whites last and fold them delicately into cake batter. Do not beat with batter, as this will cause them to lose their fluffiness. It is also advisable to keep eggs at room temperature for a while before beating them.

4. Brown sugar can be substituted for white sugar when so indicated in the recipe.

5. After greasing a baking pan, put a tablespoon of flour in it, shake it well, turn it upside down, and empty out excess flour. This will prevent cake from sticking to pan.

6. Preheat oven and put cake in as soon as oven indicator or thermometer shows temperature required.

7. In order to see if cake is ready, stick a toothpick in it. If no dough clings to it, the cake is ready to come out of the oven. Detach cake lightly from sides of pan with a knife blade, let cool for a few minutes, and take out of pan and place on wire rack. For baked custard or pudding, insert a knife in the center. If it comes out clean, it is done.

8. Cool cakes and cookies completely before storing. Cakes with custard filling or sugar and egg white icing should be kept in refrigerator.

Italian Dessert Wines

THE ANCIENT GREEKS, who appreciated good wine, called Italy *Oenotria*, the "Land of Wine." Wine was produced and consumed in large quantity all over Italy; vineyards were planted by the Romans for their conquering armies in Gaul, in Iberia, along the Rhine and the Danube, and on the eastern coast of the Adriatic. The art of wine making flourished in Italy all through the phases of its civilization. Drinking wines of the most varied types and of excellent quality was part of every festivity and banquet in the Italian courts. References to vines and wines are found in several literary works of all times. While it is not quite correctly said that on account of the lavishness with which the Italian soil produces vines everywhere Italians were always more concerned with quantity than quality, it is true that the best wines were mostly kept for local consumption. It is only in relatively recent times that Italian wines other than Chianti, Asti Spumante, and a few others already famous abroad have been exported all over the world under the protective label D.O.C. (Denominazione di Origine Controllata), which assures the consumer of the good quality of the wine he wants to buy.

The following list includes the best-known dessert wines, most of which can be found in this country—not all necessarily sweet; some, like the dry and aromatic, are in my opinion more suitable to sweeter and richer desserts.

NAME	TYPE	ALCOHOLIC CONTENT

Piedmont and Liguria

NAME	TYPE	ALCOHOLIC CONTENT
Barbera Dolce	red, sweet	11–12%
Erbaluce di Caluso Passito	red, sweet	13%
* Moscato Naturale d'Asti	golden yellow, sweet, deliciously fruity	10.5%
* Moscato d'Asti	golden yellow, sweet, deliciously fruity	11.5%
* Moscato d'Asti Spumante	golden yellow, sweet, sparkling	11.5%
Malvasia di Casorzo d'Asti	red, sweet, slightly spicy	10.5%
Nebbiolo d'Alba	red, sweet, to be served below room temperature	12%
Brachetto d'Acqui	red, sweet	11.5%
Sciacchetrà delle Cinqueterre	golden yellow, slightly sweet, with a delicate bouquet	14%

Lombardy

NAME	TYPE	ALCOHOLIC CONTENT
Bonarda dell'Oltrepo Pavese	light yellow, sweet, aromatic	10–12%
Pinot dell'Oltrepo Pavese	light yellow, dry and delicate	11%

* Indicates wines readily available in United States.

NAME	TYPE	ALCOHOLIC CONTENT

Veneto

NAME	TYPE	ALCOHOLIC CONTENT
Cabernet del Friuli	red, aromatic	12–13%
Malvasia Dolce Istriana	golden yellow, sweet, aromatic	14–15%
Moscato Istriano	golden yellow, sweet, aromatic	13–14%
Moscato dei Colli Euganei (Colli Euganei Bianco)	straw yellow, slightly sweet	10.5%
Recioto di Soave Passito	pale gold, semisweet, slight almond flavor	14–15%
Vin Santo (made with grapes hung to dry until late December)	red, very sweet, delicate muscatel flavor	15–16%

Emilia-Romagna

NAME	TYPE	ALCOHOLIC CONTENT
Albana di Romagna Amabile	golden yellow, semisweet, fruity	12–15%
* *Lambrusco*	red, slightly sweet, sparkling, to be served below room temperature	11%

Tuscany

NAME	TYPE	ALCOHOLIC CONTENT
Aleatico di Portoferraio	straw yellow, aromatic	12–15%
Moscato d'Elba	golden yellow, aromatic	14–15%
Vin Santo	red, very sweet	15–16%

* Indicates wines readily available in United States.

NAME	TYPE	ALCOHOLIC CONTENT
Marche		
Verdicchio di Matelica	light yellow green, dry or slightly sweet, aromatic	12%
Abruzzi		
* Verdicchio di Jesi	light yellow green, slightly sweet, sparkling	12%
Lazium		
Colli Albani	light to dark yellow, dry or slightly sweet, fruity	11.5%
Est! Est! Est! Abboccato di Montefiascone	pale straw yellow, slightly sweet	11%
Falerno	light yellow, aromatic	11.5%
Puglia		
Aleatico di Puglia	straw yellow, aromatic	14–17%
Moscato di Trani	golden yellow, sweet	15–17%
Calabria		
Moscato di Calabria	golden yellow, sweet	15–16%
Greco di Gerace	light yellow, semi-sweet	14–18%

* Indicates wines readily available in United States.

Sicily

Sicily has a preeminent place among the regions of Italy
in the growing and preparation of dessert wines, which goes
back to the Greek invasion of the island. In the days of the
Roman Empire Sicily was already exporting wines of the
highest quality made from grapes ripened in its blazing sun,
from the snow-covered slopes of Etna to the hot dry land
facing the northern African coast. Although quite high in
alcoholic content, the Sicilian wines have a lightness of body
which is a credit to the wine makers' skill.

NAME	TYPE	ALCOHOLIC CONTENT
* Malvasia delle Lipari	amber, aromatic	14–16%
Mamertino	golden, hearty	13.5%
* Marsala (the most famous of all dessert wines, it became very popular in Victorian times and is often preferred to Madeira, Port, or Sherry)	dark amber, aromatic, velvety, dry or sweet	16–20%
* Moscato di Noto	golden yellow, aromatic	14–15%
* Moscato di Pantelleria	golden yellow, aromatic	15–16%
* Moscato di Zucco (near Palermo)	golden yellow, aromatic	14–15%

Sardinia

NAME	TYPE	ALCOHOLIC CONTENT
Giro di Sardegna	red, similar to Port	15–16%
* Malvasia Sarda	amber, aromatic	15–18%
* Moscato Sardo	golden yellow, aromatic	15–18%

* Indicates wines readily available in United States.

Basic Doughs

Pasta Frolla
(SHORT CRUST PASTRY)

1¾ cups flour
½ cup sugar
pinch of salt

½ cup butter
1 egg and 1 yolk

Sift together flour, sugar, and salt on pastry board. Make a well in center and add butter, egg, and egg yolk. Mix, knead, and roll dough into a smooth ball, using the tips of your fingers or the heel of your hand—not the palm—and taking care not to handle too much, which makes the butter seep through. It is not necessary to add water. Chill dough in refrigerator for about 30 minutes before using.

The *pasta frolla* is used in a variety of desserts in combination with fruit preserves, fresh fruit, nuts, custard, and cheese, for pies and tarts. The most popular is the *crostata*, which is very similar to the American pie.

The recipe I've given here is more than adequate for all the desserts in the book—in fact, you will nearly always have some dough left over. When this happens, store the remaining dough, wrapped in wax paper and foil, in your freezer. Leftover dough makes wonderful impromptu cookies and tartlets, and can be used for the delicious *dolcetti di mandorle* on p. 43.

Pasta Sfoglia
(FLAKY PASTRY)

2 cups flour   ice water
pinch of salt   1 cup butter
1 egg (optional)

Sift 1½ cups of the flour with the salt on pastry board. Make a well in center, add egg, and mix, adding enough ice water to make a rather consistent dough. Knead for a few minutes, then chill half an hour. Mix together remaining flour and butter separately. Wrap in foil and chill.

Roll out the first dough mixture into a rectangular sheet. Then roll out butter-flour mixture into another rectangle; it should be almost as wide as the first dough, but only ⅔ as long. Place the butter-flour rectangle on top of the dough in such a way that a "flap" of dough is left uncovered at one end. Fold this flap over the butter mixture, then bring the other end of the dough up to cover the flap. The dough should now resemble a letter that has been folded. Turn the dough so that the short end is facing you and roll it out again. Fold it three times, like a letter, as before.

Chill 30 minutes. Repeat procedure two more times until the dough is ready to be used.

The *pasta sfoglia* is used in combination with *crema pasticcera* (thick "pastry custard," or pastry cream, p. 97), or chocolate pudding and as the basis for the Saint-Honoré, a dessert with a French name, but as essential to an Italian banquet or festive dinner as the Asti Spumante (a sweet Italian champagne). The Saint-Honoré consists of a layer of *pasta sfoglia* on which a number of cream puffs are heaped. The cream puffs may be stuffed with custard, chocolate pudding, or *zabaione* (a Marsala wine sauce), and are covered with a thin layer of caramel sugar.

Pan di Spagna
(ITALIAN SPONGE CAKE)

6 eggs, separated	1 cup flour
1 cup powdered sugar	½ tsp. baking powder
1 tsp. grated lemon rind	

Beat egg yolks and sugar in mixing bowl until lemon colored. Add lemon rind. Aside, beat egg whites until stiff and fold gently into yolks. Add sifted flour and baking powder to cake batter and pour into a greased and floured 9″ square pan. Bake at 325° for 40 minutes.

The *pan di spagna* is used very much like the *pasta sfoglia* with layers of lemon custard or chocolate pudding, or canned, frozen, or fresh fruit.

Fruit Cakes and Cookies

Crostata di Albicocche
(APRICOT PIE)

This is a delicate dessert in which the slightly tart taste
of the apricots predominates, mellowed by custard. It is also
very simple and elegant visually, with the stress on the shiny
yellow color of the apricot halves. Both it and the variation
below are excellent for a formal dinner. They could be served
with a muscatel wine from the Veneto (Colli Euganei Bianco).

Dough:
See recipe for pasta frolla,
p. 3.

Filling:

2 lb. apricots	2½ cups milk
3 egg yolks	1 lemon peel
¾ cup sugar	3 ladyfingers
1 tsp. flour	

After making dough, roll it out lightly, rounding edges, and cut, using an 8″ or 9″ pie pan as a guide, and keeping dough about 1″ larger than the pan. Grease and flour pan; line with dough. Prick dough with fork; flute edges; butter bottom surface of dough.

Wash apricots and cut in half; remove pits. Beat egg yolks with sugar and flour. Add milk and lemon peel, and cook in double boiler until slightly thickened. Remove from heat and let cool. Crush ladyfingers and sprinkle crumbs on buttered bottom of pastry-lined pan. Remove lemon peel and pour custard into pie shell. Add apricot halves upside down; sprinkle with sugar. Bake at 325° for 40 minutes.

In a dressier version of this pie, the addition of whipped cream mellows the taste of the apricots even more, and the whiteness of the cream contrasts sharply with the bright reds or blues of berries.

Follow the same recipe for dough and custard. After lining baking pan with dough, prick thoroughly with fork. Bake until golden brown, about 8–10 minutes, at 450°. Cool; place on serving dish. Cook apricot halves until soft with ½ cup sugar and enough water to cover. Remove from heat and cool. Pour custard into baked shell; add apricots, insides up. Fill with whipped cream and decorate with small strawberries, raspberries, or blueberries.

Crostata di Albicocche con Mandorle
(APRICOT ALMOND PIE)

This is a simplified version of the apricot pie, which brings out better the flavor of the apricots. The combination of apricots and almonds is very pleasant to the palate and the eyes.

Dough:
See recipe for pasta frolla,
p. 3.

Filling:
3 *ladyfingers*   2 *lb. apricots*
1½ *cups ground blanched*
   almonds

Make the dough and roll it out lightly; line greased and floured 9″ pan. Prick with fork.

Flute edges and sprinkle bottom with crumbs of ladyfingers mixed with ½ cup ground almonds. Wash apricots and cut in half; remove pits. Spread apricot halves, insides up, over 1 cup ground almonds, placing an almond in each half. Bake at 350° for 40 minutes.

Dolce di Banane e Noci Marcella
(MARCELLA'S BANANA NUT CAKE)

This recipe was given to me by one of the first Italian women I made friends with after I came to this country as a young bride. Marcella is the sensitive and warm-hearted wife of the brilliant Italian Consul in Los Angeles, Mario Ungaro, whom his California friends remember with deep friendship and admiration. Their home was a place of both intellectual stimulation and relaxation—and also of good food. One of Marcella's specialties, and a favorite of mine, was this banana nut cake which she used to serve with afternoon tea or coffee.

1¾ cups flour	⅔ cup sugar
3 tsp. baking powder	⅓ cup butter
pinch salt	2 eggs
½ cup chopped walnuts	1 cup mashed bananas
½ cup chopped dates	

Sift flour, baking powder, and salt. Flour nuts and dates so that they will not stick together. Cream sugar and butter; add eggs one at a time. Fold in bananas and sifted ingredients alternately by tablespoons. Grease 8½″ × 4½″ × 3″ pan; line with waxed paper. Pour in batter. Bake 1 hour and 10 minutes at 350°. Cut cake in squares to serve.

Sfogliata di Banane
(BANANA FLAKY PASTRY CAKE)

A very delicately flavored dessert, this banana cake is quite suitable for a formal dinner and should be accompanied by Asti Spumante, a sweet sparkling wine from Piedmont which has the rich aroma of muscat grapes.

Dough:
See recipe for pasta sfoglia,
p. 4.
Additional ingredients:
    1 *egg yolk*

Filling:

8 *bananas*	3 *egg yolks*
2 *tbsp. Kirsch*	¾ *cup sugar*
1 *lemon*	8 *tbsp. Marsala wine*

Make a dough following recipe for *pasta sfoglia*; divide into two pieces. Roll out each piece to a thickness of about ¼″, rounding edges. Brush one piece with one beaten egg yolk. Place both pieces on baking sheet brushed with water. Bake at 400° for about 25 minutes.

Slice bananas very thin and put into bowl with Kirsch. Grate the rind of the lemon, and add rind to banana mixture. Place 2 egg yolks in double boiler with sugar and beat until creamy. Add Marsala wine and cook for about 10 minutes at low heat, continuing beating until thick. Remove from heat and cool. Place unglazed baked *sfoglia* on a plate and top with half the wine sauce. Cover with bananas, remaining sauce, and baked *sfoglia* glazed with yolk.

Torta di Ciliege
(CHERRY TART)

This simple tart, something like a cobbler, is extremely easy to make, very tasty, juicy, and appealing both to adults and children. It is excellent for a family dinner, afternoon snack or tea, and might even be a welcome change in a breakfast diet of cereals or bacon and eggs.

2 *lb. fresh bing cherries*	2½ *cups pastry flour*
1 *cup granulated sugar*	2 *tsp. baking powder*
½ *cup butter*	½ *cup milk*
⅓ *cup brown sugar*	*grated rind of ½ lemon*
4 *eggs*	*pinch of salt*

Wash cherries; place in pan with enough water to cover and ¼ cup granulated sugar. Cook until mixture comes to a boil. Remove from heat; let cool in pan. Drain; remove pits. Grease 9″ × 3″ baking pan generously with butter; sprinkle with brown sugar, covering bottom evenly. Top with cherries. Melt ½ cup butter. Beat eggs and ¾ cup granulated sugar together; add flour, baking powder, milk, melted butter, lemon rind, and salt. Pour this mixture over cherries. Bake at 350° for 40–50 minutes. Turn upside down on serving plate and serve warm or cold.

Rotolo di Ciliege
(CHERRY ROLL)

This requires a little more work and ability than the preceding cherry dessert since the dough has to be rolled out and rolled up, but it is worth the effort of making it. It is even more juicy and delicious than the other, and it can be served at a formal dinner with a Moscato d'Elba.

4 lb. bing cherries	*½ cup butter*
3¼ cups sifted flour	*pinch of salt*
2½ tsp. baking powder	*½ cup milk*
1 cup granulated sugar	

Wash cherries; dry and remove pits. Sift together flour and baking powder. Add ½ cup sugar to the butter and salt and as much lukewarm milk as needed to make a soft dough. Roll out dough in a rectangular shape about ½″ thick. Boil leftover sugar for 5 minutes with ½ glass water to make a syrup. Set aside. Melt 1 tbsp. butter and pour over dough. Cover with cherries. Roll up lengthwise; cut roll in nine slices and place in buttered pan. Pour on hot syrup. Bake at 325° for about 35 minutes. May be served either warm or hot.

Crostata di Ciliege
(CHERRY PIE)

This dessert is not a classic *crostata* since I use fresh fruit in it and do not crisscross the dough on top. It tastes very rich, although actually it is not richer than the preceding cherry cakes. It is a good dinner dessert as long as light food is served. A suggested wine is the light ruby red Malvasia d'Asti, sweet and slightly spicy.

Dough:
See recipe for pasta frolla,
p. 3.

Filling:
4 lb. bing cherries	*4 ladyfingers*
¾ cup almonds	

Make a dough following the recipe for *pasta frolla*. Roll out lightly, rounding edges. Cut, keeping dough about 1″ larger than an inverted 8″ or 9″ baking pan. Butter pan and line with dough. Prick with fork and flute edges.

Wash cherries; dry and remove pits. Grind almonds, crush ladyfingers, and sprinkle crumbs and ground almonds on bottom of pastry-lined pan. Cover with cherries. Bake at 350° for about 40 minutes.

Maddalena alle Fragole
(STRAWBERRY MADDALENA)

In Italy, in the late spring and all through July, you can find the *fragoline*, tiny and deliciously flavored wood strawberries, in the markets. Although the best way of eating them is just with sugar and a little lemon juice, they are often used for desserts such as this Maddalena.

The cake for the Maddalena can be made a day ahead and the filling and topping a few hours before serving. Set the finished dessert in the refrigerator and take out 15 or 20 minutes before bringing it to the table. It is a very attractive dessert, suitable for a formal dinner and also for a buffet if it does not have to stand around too long before being served. A Muscatel wine from Tuscany or Piedmont, such as Moscato d'Elba or Moscato d'Asti, or a Moscato bianco from the Veneto, would be very appropriate.

Dough:

4 eggs, separated
½ cup sugar
¼ cup flour

2 tbsp. butter
grated rind of ½ lemon

Filling and decoration:

2 lb. small strawberries
1¼ cups powdered sugar
9 tbsp. Kirsch

1 lemon
1 cup whipping cream

Beat egg yolks with sugar until stiff; add flour, butter, and grated lemon rind and beat some more. Beat egg whites and fold into mixture. Pour into buttered and floured spring pan. Bake at 325° for 40 minutes. Cool. Place on serving dish.

Wash and drain strawberries. Add 2 tbsp. powdered sugar, 3 tbsp. Kirsch and juice of 1 lemon. Mix well and set aside. When cake is cool, put half the strawberries into blender or through sieve. Place in bowl and fold in whipped cream and remaining powdered sugar. Slice cake in half; moisten bottom half with 3 tbsp. Kirsch diluted in water. Spread with half the cream mixture and cover with half the strawberries. Top with upper half of cake. Moisten with leftover 3 tbsp. Kirsch diluted in water; cover with rest of cream and strawberries.

Crostata di Fragole con Crema
(STRAWBERRY CREAM PIE)

This dessert is very easy to make and is always sure of a warm reception. It can be prepared in the morning for that evening if custard is used. If whipped cream is used instead, it is advisable to add the strawberries an hour before serving and leave the pie in the refrigerator until then. I would serve it as a dinner dessert with a semisweet Verdicchio di Matelica.

Dough:
    See recipe for pasta frolla,
    p. 3.

Filling:

2 *lb. small strawberries*	1 *tsp. flour*
3 *tbsp. Kirsch or rum*	1 *tsp. cornstarch*
1 *cup sugar*	2¼ *cups milk*
3 *egg yolks*	1 *lemon peel*

Make a dough following the recipe for *pasta frolla*. Roll out lightly, rounding edges. Cut, keeping dough about 1″ larger than an inverted 8″ or 9″ baking pan. Grease pan; line with pastry. Flute edges; prick with fork. Bake until golden brown, about 8–10 minutes, at 450°. Cool; place on serving dish.

Wash strawberries; place in bowl with Kirsch and ¼ cup sugar diluted in some water. Set aside. Beat rest of sugar with egg yolks. Add flour, cornstarch, milk, and lemon peel, and cook in double boiler until thickened. When custard is cold, remove lemon peel. Pour custard into pastry shell. Cover with strawberries, drained, and sprinkle with sugar.

Note: Whipped cream may be substituted for custard.

Crostata di Lamponi
(RASPBERRY PIE)

The addition of the raspberries makes this dessert, which has a delicious and unusual blending of flavors, even more colorful and attractive. I recommend it to anyone who is adventurous in taste. It could be served together with a red Cabernet from Friuli, which has the fragrance of raspberries.

Dough:
See recipe for pasta frolla,
p. 3.

Filling:
4 apples	*2 lb. raspberries*
¼ cup granulated sugar	*¾ cup powdered sugar*
1 lemon	*apricot or cherry liqueur*
4 tbsp. apricot jam	

Make a dough following the recipe for *pasta frolla*. Roll out lightly, rounding edges. Cut, keeping dough about 1″ larger than an inverted 8″ or 9″ baking pan. Butter pan; line with dough.

Peel apples; slice and cook at slow heat with granulated sugar, about ½ glass water, and the peel from half the lemon. Remove apples from heat when water has evaporated; remove lemon peel, mix well and let cool. Fold in 4 tbsp. apricot jam. Fill pastry-lined pan with mixture. Bake at 325° for about 40 minutes.

Wash and drain raspberries; place in bowl. Add powdered sugar and liqueur and put in refrigerator. When pastry is ready and cool, place on serving dish, top with strawberries and, if desired, decorate with whipped cream.

Crostata al Limone
(LEMON PIE)

What makes this dessert different from the American lemon pie is not only the dough, which is sweet and crunchy, but the absence of any kind of cornstarch or gelatine. The baking procedure is also a departure from the American style. It is an excellent and unusual dessert to serve for dinner with a delicately flavored Verdicchio di Jesi.

Dough:
See recipe for pasta frolla,
p. 3.

Filling:
4 eggs, separated	*2 lemons*
¼ cup sugar	

Make a dough following the recipe for *pasta frolla*. Roll out lightly, rounding edges; cut, keeping dough about 1″ larger than an inverted 9″ baking pan. Butter and flour pan and line with dough.

Beat egg yolks and sugar well. Place in double boiler with grated peel and juice of lemons. Cook at slow heat, mixing constantly until thickened. Remove mixture from heat. Cool; fold in well-beaten egg whites. Place whole mixture in pastry-lined pan. Bake at 350° for about 40 minutes. Serve cold.

Sfogliata di Mele
(APPLE FLAKY PASTRY TURNOVER)

This is a delicious, very light dessert. It somewhat resembles its Austrian counterpart, the strudel, in appearance,
but it is much more delicate. Serve as a coffee cake for breakfast or afternoon tea.

Dough:
  See recipe for pasta sfoglia,
  p. 4.

Filling:
  2½ lb. apples   2 tbsp. cognac
  3 tbsp. butter   1 egg
  ¼ cup granulated sugar   1 tbsp. powdered sugar
  1 tsp. vanilla extract

Make a dough following the recipe for *pasta sfoglia.* Roll
out, rounding edges, to a thickness of about ¼". Place on
baking sheet.

Wash and peel apples and cut in thin slices. Place in a
saucepan with butter and cook at medium heat until soft.
Put into bowl; sprinkle with granulated sugar, vanilla, and
cognac and set aside. When cool, place on half of pastry and
fold other half over. Close well by pinching edges. Brush
pastry with slightly beaten egg. Bake at 325° for about ½
hour. Five minutes before removing from oven, sprinkle
sfogliata with powdered sugar. Serve cold.

Torta di Mele Luciana
(LUCIANA'S APPLE TART)

This recipe was given to me by my Venetian friend Luciana when we were both in our teens. It is one of the first recipes I wrote down in my oldest desserts notebook. I have never since found another apple cake like this one. It looks and tastes like solidified apple jam, but it has a far superior flavor, enhanced by the Marsala, rum, and vanilla. It is very rich and sweet; I would not recommend it as an ending to a large dinner. It is more suitable for a buffet, cut in small wedges.

2 lb. apples	*2 eggs*
4 tbsp. Marsala wine	*1 tsp. vanilla*
2 tbsp. butter	*2 tbsp. rum*
14 tbsp. sugar	*1 grated lemon rind*
6 tbsp. flour	

Peel apples and slice very thin. Cook at slow heat with Marsala, butter, and 6 tbsp. sugar. When mixture reaches consistency of a rather thick preserve, put aside and let cool. Separately, mix flour with eggs; add 6 tbsp. sugar and vanilla. Blend into apple preserve; add rum and mix well. Pour into well-greased and floured 9″ baking pan. Smooth surface with a knife and spread with grated lemon rind mixed with 2 tbsp. sugar. Bake at 325° for about 45 minutes. Serve cold.

Torta di Mele
(APPLE TART)

This is one of my favorite recipes. It is very easy to make and can be used as an excellent afternoon snack for children or adults. It can also be served for breakfast. Most of the fruit desserts which follow can be used the same way.

¾ cup raisins	¼ cup butter
¼ cup brandy	½ cup blanched almonds
1 cup flour	3 lb. apples
½ cup sugar	1 lemon
2 eggs	2 tbsp. butter

Wash raisins and soak in brandy. Make a soft dough with flour, ¼ cup sugar, 1 egg, and ¼ cup butter. Set aside. Grind almonds. Peel apples and slice very thin; place in layers in well-buttered and floured baking pan at least 3″ deep. Sprinkle raisins, grated lemon rind, little pieces of butter and sugar between each layer. When pan is full, roll out dough to size of upper part of pan; place on top of apples. Brush with remaining egg, slightly beaten. Bake at 350° for about 40 minutes.

Torta di Mele alla Campagnola
(APPLE TART COUNTRY STYLE)

This recipe, one of my very first, goes back to the postwar years, when the still extreme scarcity of such luxury items as sugar, eggs, and butter was matched only by our ingenuity in finding new ways of making desserts that, although not elegant or elaborate, were certainly satisfying. This tart is very tasty and easy to make, and is not fattening. Its texture and flavor are provided essentially by the apples, since the flour is just enough to hold the layers of apples together.

5 *tbsp. white flour*	2½ *lb. apples*
5 *tbsp. yellow cornflour*	¼ *cup butter*
5 *tbsp. sugar*	

Mix together white flour, cornflour, and sugar in a bowl. Peel apples and slice very thin. Place one layer of apples in a 9″ baking pan, sprinkle it with the flour mixture, and dot with little pieces of butter. Continue in this fashion, ending with a layer of apples; pour melted butter on top. Bake at 325° for 40 minutes.

Crostata di Mele
(APPLE PIE)

In the *Crostata di lamponi* (p. 18), apples served only as a juicy addition to raspberries. Here they are the main ingredients of the *crostata*. Both this recipe and its variation below are very good and easy to make, the latter being more moist on account of the crust covering the apples.

Dough:
See recipe for pasta frolla,
p. 3.

Filling:
2½ *lb. apples*	1 *tsp. sugar*
2 *tbsp. apricot preserve*	

Make a dough following the recipe for *pasta frolla*. Roll out lightly, rounding edges. Cut, keeping dough about 1″ larger than inverted 8″ or 9″ baking pan. Butter and flour pan; line with dough.

Peel apples and slice very thin. Spread apricot preserve on bottom of pastry-lined pan; cover with slices of apples, arranged in concentric circles, overlapping each other. Sprinkle with sugar. Bake at 325° for 35 minutes.

Variation: Follow recipe above, but cover apples with top crust into which slits have been cut. Bake at 325° for 40 minutes or until crust is golden brown.

Rotolo di Mele
(APPLE ROLL) *Fair*

This apple roll very much resembles the strudel in appearance and filling. Its dough has more consistency, though, and the filling is richer on account of the walnuts. It is easy to make and very tasty.

¾ cup raisins	2 eggs
1 tsp. powdered sugar	¼ lb. butter
2 tbsp. rum	pinch of salt
3½ cups flour	1½ cup walnuts
2 tsp. yeast	2½ lb. apples
¾ cup granulated sugar	1 grated lemon rind

Place raisins in small bowl with 1 tsp. powdered sugar; soak in rum. Place ½ cup flour in another bowl; add yeast diluted in water and as much lukewarm water as necessary to make a soft dough. Cover with a cloth and let rise for 1½ hours.

Mix rest of flour with half the sugar; 1 egg; half the butter, melted; and salt. Add yeast dough and knead well until dough is smooth and elastic. Place in floured bowl, cover with a cloth, and let rise until double, about 45 minutes.

Chop walnuts; peel apples and slice thin. Place walnuts and apples in bowl with raisins, drained; remaining sugar; and grated lemon rind. Mix well. Roll dough into oblong shape about ¼″ thick. Spread with mixture of apples, raisins, and nuts; roll up. Brush with slightly beaten egg. Bake at 350° for about 40 minutes. Let cool before slicing.

Crostata di Pere
(PEAR PIE)

This is a dessert which can very well be used for a formal dinner. The pears and the lemon custard give it a delicate, fresh taste, and the arrangement of the pear wedges makes it very attractive. A suitable wine to be served with it is Asti Spumante.

Dough:
> *See recipe for* pasta frolla,
> *p. 3.*

Filling:

2 eggs	4 large pears
½ cup sugar	1 candied cherry
¼ cup flour	½ pint whipping cream
2 cups milk	(optional)
1 lemon peel	1 tsp. vanilla extract
1 cup macaroon crumbs	(optional)

Make a dough following the recipe for *pasta frolla*. Roll out lightly, rounding edges. Cut, keeping dough about 1″

larger than inverted 9" baking pan. Butter and flour pan; line with dough.

Place eggs, sugar, and flour in a double boiler; beat well. Add milk and lemon peel. Cook at low heat, always mixing, until thickened. Remove from heat. Take out lemon peel and pour into a bowl and let cool. Add half the macaroon crumbs; sprinkle bottom of pastry-lined pan with remainder. Wash, drain and peel pears; cut in half, remove cores, and slice into wedges. Pour custard into pan and top with pear wedges arranged in circle; place a candied cherry in center. Bake at 350° for about 40 minutes. Serve cold and, if desired, with whipped cream to which 1 tsp. vanilla extract has been added.

Torta di Pere e Mele
(PEAR AND APPLE TART)

Even a child could easily make this dessert and be sure it would come out right. The sweetness and delicate flavor of the pears is a welcome addition to the tartness of the apples.

½ cup flour
4 tbsp. melted butter
6 tbsp. sugar
1 egg
1 tsp. baking powder
grated rind of ½ lemon

½ cup milk
2 pears
2 apples
¾ cup fine macaroon crumbs

Place flour, melted butter, 4 tbsp. sugar, egg, baking powder, lemon rind, and milk in a bowl and mix well.

Peel pears and apples; remove cores and slice finely. Pour cake batter into a greased and floured 9" Pyrex pan; cover alternately with slices of pears and apples. Sprinkle with rest of sugar and macaroon crumbs. Bake at 325° for about 50 minutes or until golden brown. Serve cool.

Torta di Pesche
(PEACH TART)

Although this tart is very attractive right side up on account of its crisp golden crust, it can be turned upside down on a serving dish, exposing the juicy little domes of the peaches. Either way, it is very good and very easy to make.

1¾ cups flour	*1 grated lemon rind*
¾ cup sugar	*1 tbsp. milk*
pinch of salt	*⅓ cup blanched almonds*
½ cup butter	*3 macaroons*
3 eggs	*2 lb. freestone peaches*

Sift together flour, ½ cup sugar, and salt on a floured board. Add butter, 1 egg, lemon rind, and milk. Knead lightly; set dough aside covered with a towel.

Grind almonds and macaroons. Wash and peel peaches. (In order to do this more easily plunge them in boiling water, then put them in cold water, for a few seconds.) Cut them in half; remove pits. Roll out dough and line greased and floured 9″ pan. Flute edges. Sprinkle bottom of pastry-lined pan with ground almonds and macaroons; cover with peach halves arranged domed side down. Beat 2 egg yolks with remaining sugar; fold in stiffly beaten egg whites; pour on top of peaches. Bake at 325° for about 40 minutes. Let tart cool before serving.

Crostata di Pesche e Riso
(PEACH AND RICE PIE)

This rather unusual recipe was given to me by Italian friends from Lombardy, where rice is practically a must in every meal. Here it has found its way into a peach pie, and the result is excellent. The chopped peaches prevent the cold rice from being sticky or mushy, and together they make a pretty white, gold, and red ensemble. This pie is very refreshing in hot weather and can be served at an informal dinner, together with a cool, ruby red Lambrusco wine.

Dough:
See recipe for pasta frolla,
p. 3.

Filling:
3 lbs. freestone peaches	2 tbsp. sugar
1 doz. bing cherries	1 small jar orange jelly
¼ cup rum or Cointreau	½ cup sugar cookie crumbs
¾ cup rice	

Wash and peel peaches. (In order to do this more easily, place them in boiling, then cold, water for a few seconds.) Cut in half and remove pits. Place in a bowl with pitted cherries. Pour liqueur over fruit; cover bowl with a plate and refrigerate for at least 1 hour. (This can also be done the day before, leaving fruit in refrigerator overnight.)

Following the recipe for *pasta frolla*, make a dough, roll out lightly, and line a buttered and floured spring pan up to ⅔ full. Prick bottom with a fork. Bake at 450° for about 8–10 minutes or until golden brown.

Cook rice; add sugar, mix, and cool. Remove crust from pan; place on serving dish. Set 15 peach halves aside; chop others finely and add to rice, together with 2 tbsp. orange jelly, and mix well. Put cookie crumbs on bottom of crust; cover with rice and chopped peaches. Place peach halves on top with insides facing down, and put cherries between peaches. Cover pie with a few spoonfuls of orange jelly well diluted with hot water, and refrigerate for about 1 hour.

Crostata di Prugne
(PRUNE PIE)

What gives this dessert its special flavor is the blending of the ingredients added to the prunes, especially the wine and the citrus rinds. It looks like any other fruit pie, but it has a rather unusual, spicy flavor.

Dough:
See recipe for pasta frolla,
p. 3.

Filling:

2 *cups prunes*	1 *grated lemon rind*
¾ *cup sugar*	1 *grated orange rind*
¾ *cup white wine*	⅓ *cup blanched almonds*

Soak prunes in water overnight.

Make a dough following the recipe for *pasta frolla*; roll out lightly, and divide into two pieces, one larger than the other. With the larger piece line a buttered and floured 9″ pan; set the other aside covered by a towel or bowl.

Drain prunes; remove pits and put in a pan with sugar, wine, and lemon and orange rinds. Cook slowly, mixing often. When fairly dry, remove from heat and let cool. Grind almonds and sprinkle over bottom of pastry-lined pan. Cover with prunes and second piece of dough cut to size of the top of pan. Seal the two pieces together by pressing with fork or fluting edges. Cut a few small slits on top. Bake at 325° for about 40 minutes or until golden brown.

Focaccine alle Prugne
(PRUNE PASTRIES)

½ cup prunes	pinch of salt
1 cup flour	3 tbsp. butter
2 tsp. baking powder	1 egg
¼ cup sugar	

Soak prunes in lukewarm water—just enough to cover—for 2 hours. Drain, remove pits, and chop very fine. Sift flour and baking powder over floured board. Add sugar, salt, melted butter, egg, and prunes and knead well, adding a little water if necessary. Flatten dough to about ½″ thickness and cut out with a round cutter or glass. Bake on a greased and floured sheet at 325° for about 15 minutes.

Serve cool with a cream made of whipped butter and honey beaten together well.

Crostata di Susine
(PLUM PIE)

Dough:
  See recipe for pasta frolla,
  p. 3.

Filling:
1½ lb. plums	5 tbsp. sugar
⅓ cup blanched almonds	

Make a dough following the recipe for *pasta frolla;* roll out lightly, rounding edges. Cut, keeping dough about 1″

larger than an inverted 9″ baking pan. Butter and flour pan and line with dough. Flute edges.

Wash and dry plums; remove pits and cut lengthwise into four pieces. Grind almonds; sprinkle over bottom of pastry-lined pan. Cover with plums, one near the other, with insides up; sprinkle with 3 tbsp. sugar. Bake at 325° for 35 minutes. Remove from oven; sprinkle remaining 2 tbsp. sugar on top and let cool.

If you don't want to go to the trouble of making a short crust dough, you can use the recipe for *pasticcini Milanesi* (Milanese Pastry) on page 136. You can substitute the plums with any other kind of fruit. While in the *crostata* above the flavor and texture of the fruit is outstanding, the texture of this second version is more doughy than fruity.

Pour the pastry batter into a buttered and floured 9″ baking pan; place the plums on top. It won't be necessary then to sprinkle them with sugar because the dough, rising while baking, will half cover them. Bake at 350° for 30–35 minutes.

Crostata di Uva
(GRAPE PIE)

Shiny green grapes on their peach-apricot background give this pie a particularly attractive appearance. It is an easy-to-make, tasty, and refreshing dessert, excellent for a summer dinner or buffet, to be served with the slightly sweet Est!Est!Est! wine from Lazium.

Dough:
See recipe for pasta frolla,
p. 3.

Filling:

- 1 lb. seedless grapes
- 1/4 cup rum or any fruit
  liqueur
- 3 freestone peaches
- 1/2 cup macaroon crumbs
- 2 tbsp. apricot preserves
- 1/2 pt. whipping cream

Make a dough following the recipe for *pasta frolla*; roll out lightly, rounding edges, and line a buttered and floured 9″ pan. Prick bottom with a fork. Bake at 450° for 8–10 minutes or until golden brown. Let cool and place on serving dish.

Wash and drain grapes; place in a bowl. Pour rum or liqueur over grapes; cover and place in refrigerator. Wash and peel peaches. (In order to do this more easily place in boiling, then in cold, water for a few seconds.) Chop finely and place in bowl with macaroon crumbs and apricot preserves. Mix well; pour mixture into baked shell. Cover with grapes. Serve decorated with whipped cream.

Dolce di Frutta Mista
(MIXED FRUIT CAKE)

This is a tasty and juicy dessert which resembles the classic English fruit cake in appearance. Any other kinds of fruit can be substituted or added to the ones in the recipe.

- 2 cups flour
- 2 tsp. baking powder
- 1 cup sugar
- pinch salt
- 3/4 cup butter
- 2 eggs
- grated rind of 2 lemons
- 1 1/2 lbs. plums
- 2 apples
- 1/2 lb. seedless grapes
- 4 ladyfingers

Sift together flour, baking powder, ¾ cup sugar, and salt on a floured board. Add butter, eggs, and half the lemon rind. Knead lightly and make a soft dough. Put aside covered with a towel.

Wash and dry plums and remove pits. Peel apples and slice finely. Wash and dry grapes. Place all fruit in a bowl and add other half of lemon rind and remainder of sugar. Divide dough into two pieces, one larger than the other. Roll out; line a greased and floured bread loaf pan with larger portion. Trim to rim of pan. Place ladyfingers on bottom and sides of pan. Fill with fruit and put smaller piece of dough on top. Seal the two pieces of dough by pressing with fork or fluting edges. Cut a few slits on top. Bake at 350° for about 40 minutes or until golden brown. Let cool before slicing.

Dolce a Ciambellina con Frutta di Stagione
(RING FRUIT CAKE)

This fruit cake was one of my first concoctions. It is very easy to make and allows the use of leftover fruit, even if slightly overripe. It was just because of these leftovers that my mother let me "invade" her kitchen and "play" at pastry making in my early teens. In spite of my family's kidding, my combination of sweet dough and fruit sauce turned out to be a great success.

Dough:
   ½ cup butter   1 cup flour
   ½ cup sugar   2 tsp. baking powder
   2 eggs

Topping:

4 *apricots*	1 *tbsp. apricot jam*
2 *peaches*	2 *tbsp. sugar*
2 *pears*	1 *lemon peel*
1 *small can pitted cherries*	

Cream butter with sugar. Add eggs, one at a time, and flour and baking powder, sifted together. Mix well and pour into a greased ring mold. Bake at 325° for about 40 minutes. Let cool.

Wash fruit and cut into medium size pieces. Put into a saucepan with jam diluted in water, sugar, and lemon peel. Cook at slow heat until soft. Remove lemon peel and let cool. If fruit compote is too watery, take out fruit, set aside in a bowl, and let juice and jam cook a little longer with more sugar added until it is thicker. Add fruit again. Place cake on a serving dish and fill the center with half the fruit. Pour the other half over cake.

Torta di Frutta e Cioccolata
(FRUIT AND CHOCOLATE TART)

When I made up this recipe, I didn't know that almost 20 years later I would find similar desserts in most health food stores in California. It is a very tasty, compact, and chewy tart, and can last even a week wrapped in aluminum foil without becoming stale—unless there is somebody in your family who loves nuts and dry fruit as much as I do.

2 *full tbsp. flour*	½ *cup milk*
2 *tbsp. cocoa*	1 *cup toasted almonds*
pinch of salt	¼ *cup dates*
2 *tbsp. butter*	¼ *cup prunes*
1 *egg*	¼ *cup dry figs*
2 *tbsp. sugar*	

Sift together flour, cocoa, and salt in a bowl. Cream butter and blend with egg beaten with sugar. Add milk and mix well. Chop almonds and dry fruit and add to batter. Mix and pour into a greased and floured 9″ round or square pan. Bake at 350° for 40–45 minutes.

Nut Cakes and Cookies

FOR MOST OF these desserts it is necessary to have a small
nut grinder, very similar to a cheese grinder, which can be
found in Italian grocery stores. You can use a blender—if
your blender will grind nuts to a consistency only a little
coarser than flour.

Amaretti
(ALMOND MACAROONS)

These cookies are also commercially made and can be
found packaged in tin boxes in most Italian grocery stores.

They are wrapped in colored tissue paper two by two, and are very crisp and light; when you bite into them they practically melt in your mouth. The homemade ones are crisp on the outside and slightly chewy inside, like coconut macaroons. Personally, I prefer them to those commercially made. They can also be sprinkled with pine nuts instead of sugar, which gives them a special extra flavor.

1½ cup blanched almonds   *2 egg whites*
2 cups powdered sugar   *½ tsp. almond extract*

Grind almonds. Add powdered sugar, less 2 tbsp.; egg whites, stiffly beaten; and almond extract. Batter should be thick enough to allow shaping of cookies by rolling mixture up in little balls. Place on well-greased and floured baking sheet, some distance from each other, and flatten slightly with palm of hand. Sprinkle with powdered sugar. Bake at 350° for about 5 minutes or until golden brown.

Bavarese alle Mandorle
(ALMOND BAVARIAN CREAM)

This recipe really belongs in Chapter VII, but I decided to include it in this chapter in order to have one nut dessert here which does not require any baking. It is absolutely delicious and can be served at a formal dinner with *amaretti* and a muscatel wine from the Veneto such as Colli Euganei Bianco.

1 cup blanched almonds   *1 package gelatine*
1 cup milk   *1 pint whipping cream*
½ cup granulated sugar   *2 tbsp. powdered sugar*
1 tsp. vanilla   *¼ cup rum*
5 egg yolks

Grind almonds. Put milk, granulated sugar, and vanilla in a double boiler and heat. Beat egg yolks and add to mixture. Cook at low heat, continuing beating until about to boil. Dilute gelatine with water and add to ingredients in double boiler; pour into a bowl to cool. Fold in ⅔ of the pint of cream, well whipped, and ground almonds, powdered sugar, and rum. Pour into an 8″, well buttered mold and leave in refrigerator 2–3 hours. Serve decorated with remaining whipped cream.

Paste alle Mandorle
(ALMOND PASTRY)

These almond cookies are the specialty of one of the best Venetian pastry shops. They are very attractive, with a shiny and golden crust and a decoration of cherries or almonds. Like the *amaretti*, they are crisp outside and a little chewy inside, and quite irresistible.

6 egg yolks (5 boiled) *pinch of salt*
¾ cup blanched almonds *grated rind of ½ lemon*
½ cup sugar   *¾ cup butter*
1¾ cups flour   *1 doz. candied cherries*
1 tsp. baking powder

Hard boil 5 eggs and let cool. Cut them in half and scoop out the yolks. Put yolks through a sieve and discard boiled egg whites. Grind half the almonds and add ¼ cup sugar. Sift flour, baking powder, and salt on a board. Add lemon rind, almonds, and sieved boiled egg yolks. Mix well and add 1 raw yolk and butter; knead lightly and set aside. Cut rest of almonds in strips and cherries in half. Roll out dough ¼″ thick and cut in round shapes with cookie cutter or glass.

Place on greased and floured baking sheet. Beat 1 egg white lightly with rest of sugar and brush onto cookies. Place a half cherry in center of each cookie and surround with almond strips. Bake at 325° for about 20 minutes or until golden brown.

Dolce di Mandorle
(ALMOND CAKE)

If you want a cake which can be kept ready for any emergency, or if you watch your diet and are allowed only a little slice a day, try this recipe. This is a cake which will keep for weeks, and is very easy to make too.

1 cup butter	*1 full cup flour*
2¾ cups powdered sugar	*1 tsp. vanilla extract*
6 eggs	*1 tsp. rum extract*
1⅓ cups blanched almonds	*1 tsp. lemon extract*

Cream butter with sugar. Hard boil 3 eggs and let cool. Cut them in half; scoop out the yolks and put them through a sieve. Discard boiled egg whites and add sieved yolks to butter mixture. Separate 3 remaining eggs, reserving the whites, and add yolks to butter mixture along with ground almonds, sifted flour, and vanilla, rum, and lemon extracts, and fold in reserved egg whites beaten stiff. Bake in a 3″ deep pan 9″ wide, well greased and floured, at 325° for about 45 minutes.

Torta di Pasta Frolla e Mandorle
(ALMOND SHORT CRUST TART)

Dough:
See recipe for pasta frolla,
p. 3.

Filling:
1 cup almonds	*½ cup powdered sugar*
2 egg whites	*1 egg yolk*

Make a dough with the recipe for *pasta frolla*. Divide into two pieces and roll out flat. Cut one piece round, the size of the bottom of a 9″ pan. Line pan with other piece of dough and trim at edges.

Grind almonds, leaving a few aside for decoration; add egg whites beaten stiff, and sugar. Spread mixture in pan and cover with round piece of dough. Brush with egg yolk; decorate with almond halves. Bake at 325° for about 40 minutes or until golden brown.

Dolcetti di Mandorle
(ALMOND COOKIES)

Since making *pasta frolla* is a somewhat laborious procedure, I always make some extra and store it in the freezer wrapped up in aluminum foil. It takes about 2 hours to defrost; then it is ready to use, as fresh as if you had just made it. You can use it to make these delicious cookies, which should be served the same day because they don't keep long on account of the custard.

Dough:
See recipe for pasta frolla,
p. 3.

Filling:
2 *eggs and 2 egg yolks*   ¼ *cup rum*
6 *tbsp. sugar*   *apricot or peach preserves*
1 *tsp. flour*   1 *cup blanched almonds*
½ *cup milk*

Make a dough following recipe for *pasta frolla* and set
aside under an inverted bowl.

Put 2 whole eggs, 2 yolks, sugar, and flour in a double
boiler; beat well and add milk. Cook, always stirring, until
custard is thickened. Remove from heat and add rum. Flatten
out dough ¼″ thick and line two greased and floured small-
cup muffin pans. Put ½ tsp. jam at bottom of each cup and
fill with custard. Place almonds, cut lengthwise in four, on
custard. Bake at 325° for about 20 minutes or until golden
brown.

Torta Secca Lauretta
(LAURETTA'S DRY TART)

My best friend Laura Gatti, who was nicknamed Lauretta,
gave me this recipe when we were in our teens. She used to
make it for her brothers and sister and their numerous friends
when we all got together for mad excursions on skis or day-
long hikes at her family's charming villa in the Veneto Alps.
It was a real treat on our return home, together with hot
coffee and *grappa*, the Alpine version of vodka.

1½ cups blanched almonds   2 egg yolks
1 cup butter   2¾ cups flour
1 cup sugar   ¼ tsp. salt

Grind almonds. Cream butter with sugar; add egg yolks, sifted flour, and salt. Add ground almonds and mix well. Spread mixture in a greased and floured 3″ deep 9″ pan. Bake at 325° for about 50 minutes.

Note: This cake can be made a day or so ahead; it improves with time.

Bocca di Dama
(MILADY'S CAKE)

The Italian name means literally "Milady's Mouth," which indicates that it is a dessert delicate enough for a lady's palate. The absence of butter or any other shortening and the number of beaten eggs, plus the ground almonds, which add a slightly grainy texture, make this cake extremely light—it practically melts in your mouth. It is a classic among Italian desserts.

½ cup blanched almonds   1 cup flour
7 eggs, separated   grated rind of ½ lemon
1 cup sugar

Grind almonds. Beat the egg yolks with sugar until creamy. Add ground almonds, flour, and grated lemon rind; mix well. Fold in stiffly beaten egg whites and put into a greased and floured 3″ deep baking pan. Bake at 325° for about 40 minutes.

Torta di Mandorle e Cioccolata
(ALMOND AND CHOCOLATE TART)

1 cup blanched almonds
3 tbsp. butter
4 squares bittersweet
  baking chocolate
½ cup milk

2 tsp. potato flour
5 eggs, separated
¾ cup sugar
1 tsp. vanilla extract

Grind almonds and place in a bowl. Melt butter and chocolate in a double boiler; add milk and potato flour. Mix well. When well blended, remove from heat and add to almonds. Let cool. Add egg yolks, beaten with sugar until creamy, and vanilla. Mix; fold in egg whites beaten stiff. Pour in a greased and floured 3″ deep baking pan. Bake at 350° for about 50 minutes.

Fave dei Morti
(COOKIES OF THE DEAD)

The mournful name of these cookies is just due to the fact that they are traditionally made on November 2, the day commemorating the dead. For the Italians every occasion is good to indulge in some special culinary treat. If one would put together all the recipes of the different desserts made in Italian towns and villages for the name-days of their patron saints, one could fill up a book at least twice the size of this one. These particular cookies are very tasty, but pretty hard —so be very careful when you bite into them.

| 1½ cups walnuts | ½ cup whole wheat flour |
| ½ cup sugar | 1½ tbsp. butter |

Grind walnuts; mix with sugar and flour on floured board. Add butter, creamed, and a little water or Marsala wine in order to make a soft dough. Divide into little pieces and shape like cylinders about 3″ long. Place on greased and floured baking sheet; flatten with palm of hand. Bake at 325° for about 30 minutes.

Torta di Nocciole
(HAZELNUT TART)

In my opinion, the taste of chocolate goes very well with that of hazelnuts. The blending of the two ingredients, together with the beaten eggs—which account for the lightness of the filling—make it a very delectable and rather unusual dessert. This tart is a little too rich, though, to serve for dinner. It is more suitable for afternoon tea or coffee and buffet.

Dough:
See recipe for pasta sfoglia,
  p. 4.

Filling:

1 cup hazelnuts	1 cup milk
¾ cup powdered sugar	2 eggs, separated
6 ounces bittersweet baking chocolate	1 tsp. vanilla extract

Make a dough following recipe for *pasta sfoglia*. Divide into two pieces and set aside, covered with a towel.

Grind hazelnuts. Melt half the sugar with chocolate and

1 tbsp. water in a double boiler. Add milk. Put hazelnuts and chocolate in a bowl. Add egg yolks, beaten with the rest of the sugar; egg whites, beaten stiff; and vanilla. Mix well. Line a 9″ pan with half the dough, rolled out flat; pour cake mixture into shell. Cover with other piece of dough cut in strips ½″ wide, crisscrossed. Bake at 325° for 40 minutes.

Torta di Cioccolato e Noci
(CHOCOLATE AND WALNUT TART)

Here, as in the preceding recipe, the addition of chocolate gives this dessert a richer taste. It is easier and faster to make than the other, but just as good. It can be served at a formal dinner because it looks very attractive, with its decoration of whipped cream and nuts, but only after a rather light main course. This tart goes well with a muscatel wine such as Asti Spumante.

3 lb. whole walnuts	*1½ cups powdered sugar*
3 oz. bittersweet baking chocolate	*1½ cups flour*
	5 eggs, separated
1 cup butter	*½ cup whipping cream*

Set aside a dozen walnut halves and grind rest. Melt chocolate in double boiler. Beat butter in a bowl until fluffy and creamy. Add sugar, flour, egg yolks, chocolate, and ground walnuts, mixing well. Beat egg whites until stiff; fold into mixture. Bake in a 3″ deep 9″ pan at 325° for 40–50 minutes. Let cool and place on a serving dish. Decorate with whipped cream and walnut halves.

Biscotti ai Pignoli
(PINE NUT COOKIES)

1¾ cups flour
pinch of salt
½ cup sugar
2 eggs plus 1 yolk

½ cup olive oil
grated rind of 1 lemon
2 tbsp. pine nuts

Place flour, salt, sugar, and 2 whole eggs in a bowl; add oil and lemon rind. Mix well. Roll out dough on a floured board to about ⅓″ thickness and cut in strips 3″ × 1″. Brush with egg yolk and sprinkle with pine nuts. Place on a greased baking sheet. Bake at 325° for 25–30 minutes.

Crostata di Pignoli
(PINE NUT PIE)

This is a rather unusual pie, possibly also the most unusual way of serving cream of wheat. Although it is very sweet and filling, you will love the taste of pinenuts in combination with the *pasta frolla* and the cream of wheat.

Dough:
  See recipe for pasta frolla,
  p. 3.

Filling:
  ¾ cup pine nuts
  2¼ cups milk
  ½ cup instant cream of
    wheat
  ¼ cup granulated sugar

  2 eggs
  1 tbsp. butter
  grated rind of ½ lemon
  pinch of salt
  ¼ cup powdered sugar

Make a dough following recipe for *pasta frolla*. Divide into two pieces and cover with a towel.

Chop pine nuts. Bring milk to boil in double boiler. Sprinkle with instant cream of wheat, continuing stirring, and let boil for 30 seconds. Remove from heat. Add granulated sugar, eggs, butter, lemon rind, salt, and pine nuts; mix well. Roll out dough on floured board and line a 9" baking pan with one piece. Trim edges. Pour in cream of wheat mixture; cover with rest of dough cut in strips ½" wide, crisscrossed. Bake at 350° for about 30 minutes. Serve sprinkled with powdered sugar.

Tartine alle Mandorle o Nocciole
(ALMOND OR HAZELNUT PASTRY)

This dessert is very easy to make when you follow the rules for *pasta frolla* well. I made this recipe up out of nostalgia for my childhood days, because its taste reminds me of the caramel nuts and fruit strung on a bit of wire or stuck on bamboo sticks which the "ometo dei caramei" (the little caramel man) used to sell around our school in Venice.

Dough:
See recipe for pasta frolla,
p. 3

Filling:
½ cup almonds or   1 tsp. caramelized
   hazelnuts   sugar
1 doz. candied cherries
   (optional)

Make a dough following recipe for *pasta frolla*. Roll out about ½" thick and cut with round cookie cutter. Line a small-cup muffin pan, greased and floured, with the dough disks. Bake at 325° for 15 minutes or until golden brown.

Remove tarts from cups and place 3 or 4 almonds or hazelnuts and a candied cherry in each. Pour 1 tsp. of hot caramelized sugar over them and let cool.

Note: To make caramelized sugar, put 4 tbsp. sugar and 2 tbsp. water in a small pan. Keep mixing until melted and golden brown. Do not let boil or it will burn and become bitter. Use immediately before it gets hard.

Nut Pastry Without Flour or Fat

Dolce di Mandorle o Noci
(ALMOND OR WALNUT CAKE)

This cake is my very favorite. First of all, it looks beautiful, like something out of a pastry shop (if you use the pastry tube to decorate it, of course). Second, when you eat it, it melts in your mouth. It rises quite a bit if baked right, but even if it doesn't—in case the egg whites are not beaten enough or have not been folded in well, or the oven is too warm—do not despair. Once you have added the whipped cream it will still look all right and taste delicious.

6 eggs, separated
6 tbsp. powdered sugar

1½ cups almonds or walnuts
1 pt. whipping cream

Beat egg yolks well with 5 tbsp. sugar; add ground almonds or walnuts and gently fold in stiffly beaten egg whites. (Leave a few nuts aside to decorate cake.) Bake at 325° for 45 minutes in a 3″ deep spring pan. Let cool and place on serving dish.

Whip cream and add 1 tbsp. sugar. Slice cake in two and place some whipped cream between layers. Cover whole cake with rest of whipped cream and decorate with almonds or walnuts.

Note: When using almonds, add 1 tsp. instant coffee to whipping cream before whipping and one more tsp. sugar.

Torta di Noci
(WALNUT TART)

Whoever likes walnuts will love this. You can very well substitute the confectioners' sugar with brown sugar: the cake will not be so light, but it will have an extra flavor and be better than the most exclusive pastry of the health food stores. A sprinkling of powdered sugar will make it more attractive.

1 cup walnuts
4 eggs, separated

1 cup confectioners' sugar
⅓ cup bread crumbs

Grind walnuts. Beat egg yolks with sugar until creamy. Add walnuts, stiffly beaten egg whites, and bread crumbs. Bake in a greased and floured 3″ deep spring pan at 325° for about 45 minutes.

Torta di Mandorle e Carote
(ALMOND AND CARROT TART)

This is definitely a health food store dessert, although dated from a time when today's health food entrepreneurs were not even born. It is excellent, and more juicy than the preceding cake because of the addition of carrots. You don't really taste the carrots, and if you didn't know that they were there, you could never tell. Therefore, you can serve it also to other than health food fans as a more elegant dessert than it is in reality.

¾ lb. fresh carrots
2 cups almonds
½ cup bread crumbs
2 tsp. baking powder
4 eggs, separated

4 tbsp. sugar
grated rind of 1 lemon
⅓ cup pine nuts
powdered sugar (optional)

Wash, drain, and grate carrots into a large bowl. Grind almonds. Add to carrots with bread crumbs, baking powder, egg yolks beaten with sugar until creamy, and grated lemon rind. Mix well; fold in stiffly beaten egg whites. Pour batter into a greased and floured 3″ deep spring pan; sprinkle with pine nuts. Bake at 325° for 50 minutes. If you wish, this can be served sprinkled with powdered sugar.

Dolce di Chiari d'Uovo e Nocciole
(HAZELNUT CAKE)

Suppose you make some marvelous *zabaione* (p. 106), which requires only egg yolks and you hate to throw away all those protein-filled egg whites. You can keep them for the next day and make this excellent cake—with or without the chocolate icing—for that is actually how my recipe originated. It is suitable for breakfast, afternoon tea or coffee, and as a children's snack.

7 egg whites	*juice of ½ lemon*
1 cup granulated sugar	*1 doz. sugar cubes*
1½ cups hazelnuts	*2 squares bittersweet*
grated rind of ½ lemon	*baking chocolate*

Beat egg whites until stiff. Add sugar and hazelnuts, finely ground, and lemon rind and juice. Bake in a 9″ greased and floured 3″ deep spring pan at 325° for about 45 minutes. Let cool. Cover with chocolate icing made by melting sugar cubes in just enough water to cover in a double boiler and adding baking chocolate, mixing until well blended.

Quarti di Luna alle Noci
(WALNUT CROISSANTS)

These cookies are delicious and very easy to make. They are ideal for afternoon tea or coffee and can be served for dinner with mousses, creams, and ice creams.

4 eggs, separated	*2 cups walnuts*
13 tbsp. sugar	

Beat egg yolks with sugar until creamy. Grind walnuts and add to yolks. Fold in well beaten egg whites. Mixture should be firm enough to shape into little croissants. Place on a well-greased and floured baking sheet. Decorate with pieces of walnuts. Bake at 325° for 20 minutes.

Fresh Fruit Desserts

Albicocche al Forno
(BAKED APRICOTS)

During apricot season there comes a time when the markets
have large quantities of this excellent fruit at a very cheap
price—on account of the fact that they get overripe so soon
and must be sold in a hurry. Therefore, this is also the time
to make all kinds of apricot desserts. In this particular recipe,
in which I use apricots very much the same way as in a
recipe for baked peaches, the slightly tart taste of apricots is
well blended with the sweetness of the Marsala wine sauce.
It is a good dessert to be served for dinner with a muscatel
wine from Sicily, such as Moscato di Noto.

1 lb. apricots
1¼ cups macaroon crumbs
1 cup sugar
4 egg yolks

3 tbsp. butter
½ cup Marsala wine
⅓ cup flour
1½ cups milk

Wash and drain apricots; cut in half and remove pits. Sprinkle a greased enamel or Pyrex 9″ pan—which can also be used to serve—with 1 tbsp. macaroon crumbs; cover with apricot halves, insides up. Fill with a mixture of macaroon crumbs, ⅓ cup sugar, 1 egg yolk, 1 tbsp. butter, and ¼ cup Marsala. Bake at 325° for 35 minutes. Let cool. Beat remaining 3 egg yolks with flour; add remaining sugar and Marsala, 2 tbsp. butter, and milk. Mix well and pour into double boiler. Keep stirring and cook until thickened. Remove from heat before mixture begins to boil; pour over apricots. Serve cool.

Coppa di Albicocche
(APRICOT CUP)

This dessert somewhat resembles the English trifle. The apricots add a fresh and aromatic taste and are very attractive in combination with the whipped cream. Use it for a formal dinner with a Malvasia Dolce Istriana.

1½ lb. apricots
1 cup sugar
⅓ cup rum
4 eggs
⅓ cup flour

1½ cups milk
1 lemon peel
1 cup whipping cream
2 doz. ladyfingers

Wash apricots. Place in a pan with ¼ cup sugar and enough water to barely cover. Cook until boiling. Remove from heat, drain, and let cool. Cut in half, remove pits and place in a bowl. Pour rum over apricots, cover bowl and place in refrigerator.

Beat eggs, the rest of the sugar, and flour in a small bowl; add milk and mix well. Pour into double boiler, add lemon peel, and cook until thickened. Remove from heat and let cool. Fold in ½ cup whipped cream. Drain rum liquid from apricots for later use; chop ⅔ of the apricots and set aside. Line bottom of a large glass bowl with some ladyfingers moistened with the rum in which apricots were soaked, and pour some custard over them. Cover with a layer of chopped apricots, more ladyfingers, and so on, ending with custard. Place apricot halves on top, some in a circle and three in the middle, insides up, and fill with remaining whipped cream. Leave in refrigerator 2–3 hours before serving.

Arance Ripiene alle Fragole
(STUFFED ORANGES WITH STRAWBERRIES)

This lovely dessert is versatile and the whipped cream and decoration, while very pretty, can be left out for a family dinner or diet-conscious friends without taking anything essential away.

6 large oranges	*⅓ cup Kirsch*
1 can strawberries,	*⅓ cup powdered sugar*
unsweetened, or 1½	*1 cup whipping cream*
cups fresh strawberries	

Wash and dry oranges. Slice off tops, scoop out; place pulp in a bowl. Chop half the pulp and put into another bowl with strawberries, liqueur, and sugar. Mix well; stuff oranges with mixture. Cover oranges with whipped cream and replace orange tops so that cream may show. Decorate with candied fruit forming stems and leaves.

Note: Stuffing can be prepared ahead of time, placed in refrigerator, and used to stuff oranges just before serving. It is a good idea to have a bowl with extra chopped oranges and strawberries to place on the table for refills. Serve this with Moscato Naturale d'Asti.

Arance Ripiene alla Crema
(STUFFED ORANGES WITH CUSTARD)

6 *large oranges*	2 *egg yolks*
¼ *cup sugar*	⅓ *cup Cointreau*
¼ *cup flour*	½ *cup whipping cream*

Wash and dry oranges, slice off tops, and place in a serving dish. Scoop out pulp and put through a sieve into a double boiler. Add sugar, flour, yolks, and liqueur beaten together. Mix well; cook until thickened. Remove from heat; let cool, and pour over oranges. Place in refrigerator; remove 20–30 minutes before serving. Decorate with whipped cream and leave in refrigerator until serving time.

Note: Instead of the whipped cream, you can just add half a maraschino cherry for decoration. Dry it well first on a paper towel, though; otherwise it will make pink drippings on the custard. This variation is a little richer and just as attractive as the basic recipe. It can be used the same way, with Moscato Naturale d'Asti.

Dolce di Banane
(BANANA CAKE)

This is a very delicate-tasting dessert, particularly suited to an elegant dinner. Instead of making *pan di Spagna*, you can speed up preparation by using commercially-made pound cake. You can also add a few maraschino cherries or blanched almonds for decoration. Serve with Pinot dell'Oltrepo Pavese from Lombardy.

6 bananas	1 tbsp. flour
⅓ cup rum	1½ cups milk
4 egg yolks	¾ lb. pan di Spagna (p. 5)
2 tbsp. sugar	or pound cake

Slice bananas finely and place in a small bowl; cover with rum diluted with a little water. Beat yolks, sugar, and flour until creamy; add milk. Cook in double boiler until thickened. Remove from heat and let cool. Drain bananas.

Slice *pan di Spagna* in half horizontally, and place bottom half in an oblong or round serving dish moistened with the liqueur in which bananas were soaked. Cover with half the bananas and the top layer of cake. Set aside, weighed down by another plate, until custard is cold. Pour custard over cake and decorate with two circles of banana slices. Keep in refrigerator until time to serve.

Montebianco
(MONT BLANC—CHESTNUT DESSERT)

The *Montebianco* is a classic Italian dessert which can be found in most Italian cookbooks with slight variations. This is my version of it. It is the easiest thing to make and very light and fluffy. The whipped cream is a very good addition to the mashed chestnuts, which by themselves would be too dry. You can substitute the whipped cream with chocolate fudge, but then, of course, you would no longer have a *Montebianco*, but a *Montenero* (Black Mountain). It is a family dessert, especially welcomed by children.

2 lb. chestnuts
pinch of salt
1 cup milk

1 tsp. vanilla extract
1 cup sugar
½ cup whipping cream

Peel chestnuts, put into a 3-qt. pan with a pinch of salt; cover with water and boil for 5 minutes. Drain, remove inner skin, and put back into pan with milk and vanilla. When they are well cooked and all the milk is absorbed, mash and add sugar. Beat well; put through a sieve onto a serving dish. Let mixture pile up in a cone-shaped mound. Cover mound with whipped cream, giving it the shape of a rugged snowy mountain. Serve chilled.

Palla di Neve
(SNOWBALL—CHESTNUT DESSERT)

This is a very delicate and attractive dessert. The addition of liqueur brings a touch of sophistication to it, and together with its white and green decoration, makes it quite suitable

for a formal dinner. It should be served with Moscato d'Asti
Spumante.

2 lb. chestnuts	¼ cup unsweetened
1 cup milk	powdered cocoa
1 cup powdered sugar	½ cup whipping cream
½ cup rum or Curaçao	¼ cup pistachio nuts

Cook the chestnuts following the procedure of the previous
recipe. Mash; add powdered sugar and liqueur. Mix well. Put
into a serving dish, giving it a semispheric shape. Chill.

Before serving, with the help of a pastry tube, decorate
dessert with little flower-shaped mounds of whipped cream
placed close to each other; place pistachio nuts between
mounds.

Castagne Glassate
(GLAZED CHESTNUTS)

The difficult thing in this recipe is to keep the chestnuts
from breaking up in little pieces. That's why the glazed chestnuts which are commercially made are sold at such a high
price. For family consumption it doesn't really matter if they
are not in one piece. They taste just as good.

1½ lb. chestnuts	¼ cup rum
1½ lb. sugar	

Peel chestnuts; put into a pan, cover with water and boil for
5 minutes. Drain; remove inner skin, put back into pan, cover
with water and cook until soft. Drain and set aside. Put sugar
in double boiler with ¾ cup water and boil until it makes
a thick syrup. Remove from heat; let cool. Add rum and
chestnuts. Mix lightly; pour onto greased serving dish, sepa-
rating chestnuts with a wet wooden spoon.

Ciliege al Marsala
(MARSALA CHERRIES)

2 lb. fresh bing cherries
1 cup sugar
1 cup white wine
1 lemon peel
4 eggs
½ cup Marsala wine

Wash cherries; cook with ¼ cup sugar, white wine, and lemon peel. Let boil 5 minutes; remove from heat and let cool. Remove pits; place cherries in a glass bowl. Put eggs and remaining sugar into a double boiler; beat well and add Marsala. Cook until thick and fluffy, continuing beating. Remove from heat and keep beating until cool. Pour over cherries; mix. Refrigerate for a couple of hours.

Note: These Marsala cherries can also be served in small glass bowls or sherbet glasses. They look very pretty—all red and gold—and are absolutely delicious. Use them for a formal dinner with *amaretti* (almond macaroons, p. 39) or *pasticcini milanesi* (Milanese pastry, p. 136) and Moscato di Trani.

Cocomero Ghiacciato
(ICED WATERMELON)

Even a child can make this very cooling dessert—not fattening and so colorful that it looks like summer itself. It is very much like watermelon ice, and it is perfect for a hot summer night.

1 small watermelon
½ cup sugar
1 tsp. vanilla extract
¼ cup chopped candied fruit

Cut watermelon in half. Scoop out pulp; strain. Add sugar, vanilla, and candied fruit. Put into a greased pudding mold or sherbet glasses and freeze.

Crema Gelata alle Fragole
(ICED STRAWBERRY CREAM)

Although this dessert sounds like vanilla ice cream with strawberries, it has a much more creamy texture. It is well suited for a formal summer dinner and should be served with Malvasia Dolce Istriana.

6 eggs, separated	*1½ pt. whipping cream*
¾ cup sugar	*2 lb. strawberries*
1 tsp. vanilla extract	*⅓ cup rum*

Put 6 egg yolks in double boiler with ½ cup sugar; beat well and cook until lukewarm. Remove from heat; pour into a bowl and add vanilla. Beat well until fluffy and cold. Fold in half of cream, well whipped, and 3 stiffly beaten egg whites. Pour mixture into round or rectangular pan lined with waxed paper. Place in freezer for a few hours.

Wash and drain strawberries. Put into a bowl; add rum and rest of sugar diluted with a little water. Put into refrigerator. About 15 minutes before serving, whip rest of cream. Remove frozen custard from freezer and cut into triangular or rectangular pieces. Serve all together on a serving plate, or on individual dishes. Decorate with strawberries and whipped cream.

Crema di Lamponi
(RASPBERRY CREAM)

This is perhaps the simplest kind of fruit dessert, very easy to make, and with a very delicate flavor. It can be used for a family or formal dinner with *amaretti* (almond macaroons, p. 39) and Recioto di Soave Passito.

2 lb. fresh raspberries   *¾ cup whipping cream*
1 lb. powdered sugar

Wash, drain, and mash raspberries. Add powdered sugar and mix well. Fold in cream, well whipped. Refrigerate a few hours and serve in sherbet glasses.

Panna di Mele
(APPLE CREAM)

This is a very light dessert, very appropriate for children, and for after a heavy meal.

4 lb. baking apples   *2 egg whites*
2 tbsp. powdered sugar

Cook apples whole with a little water. Peel, remove cores, and put through a sieve or into a blender. Add sugar and well-beaten egg whites; mix well. Continue beating until mixture has consistency of whipped cream. Serve chilled in sherbet glasses.

Frittelle di Mele
(APPLE FRITTERS)

These fritters are excellent for breakfast, or for an afternoon snack. I made them once for a group of four adults and twelve children and teenagers with whom I was sharing a cabin during the ski season at Mammoth, California. We adults were taking turns at cooking breakfast and dinner, so when it came to my turn for breakfast I thought I would surprise everyone by serving them something they had never had before. The fritters were a great success, but I kept on frying for an hour because the more I made the more they asked for. Consequently, after that experience I decided to stick to more conventional breakfasts when it came to feeding a rather large number of hungry skiers.

5 apples	*¼ cup cognac*
4 tbsp. powdered sugar	*2 tbsp. flour*

Peel and core apples; cut in ¼″ slices the shape of a doughnut. Place in a bowl, sprinkle with 2 tbsp. sugar, and pour cognac over. Set aside for one hour, turning over once. Drain; dip in a rather thin batter made with flour and some water. Fry in deep hot fat until golden brown. Serve sprinkled with remaining sugar.

Note: Sliced oranges, peaches, or figs cut in half can be used instead of apples.

Mele al Forno
(BAKED APPLES)

6 *Rome Beauty apples*   *3 tbsp. sugar*
6 *tbsp. raspberry or*
    strawberry jam or
    marmalade

Wash and drain apples. Core; place in an 11¾″ × 7½″ buttered Pyrex baking pan. Put 1 tbsp. jam in each center; sprinkle a little sugar on top. Bake at 350° for about 45 minutes.

Note: Half a cup of raisins soaked for about 30 minutes in rum can be used instead of jam.

Mele Meringate
(MERINGUED APPLES)

This is a surprise dessert. Nobody expects to find an apple under that soft white mound of meringue. I recommend them instead of the usual candied apples, surely worse than these for children's teeth. In fact, I made them for the first time for my own children as a substitute for the candied ones which I had refused to buy them at their school's carnival.

6 *Rome Beauty apples*   *3 egg whites*
¾ *cup sugar*   *6 candied cherries*

Peel and core apples. Cook in enough water to cover and ¼ cup sugar until soft. Drain; place on a buttered baking pan. Beat egg whites stiff, gradually adding rest of sugar.

Cover each apple with meringue and decorate with cherries cut in half. Bake at 500° for 3–5 minutes, until meringue is light gold. Serve immediately.

Melone Ghiacciato Ripieno
(ICED STUFFED MELON)

This delightful dessert is very suitable for a summer buffet.

1 large cantaloupe or other melon	*½ lb. raspberries or strawberries*
½ pineapple	*½ cup sugar*
	½ cup Cointreau or rum

Slice off upper part of melon and set aside. Scoop out and discard seeds. Remove pulp and place in a bowl. Add pineapple, chopped, and raspberries, well washed and drained. Sprinkle with sugar and pour Cointreau over. Mix all the fruit well and put into melon bottom. Cover with upper part and seal with a little butter. Leave in refrigerator a few hours before serving.

Pere alla Crema e Zabaione
(PEARS WITH CREAM AND ZABAIONE)

This is a very delicate dessert, well suited for a formal dinner party to be served with Moscato d'Asti.

6 large pears	*3 candied cherries*
4 tbsp. sugar	

Peel and core pears. Cook until soft in enough water to cover and sugar (about 15 minutes). Drain and place on a serving dish. Fill centers with *crema pasticcera* (pastry cream, p. 97) and cover with *zabaione* (p. 106). Decorate with candied cherries cut in half. Serve cold.

Pere Ripiene al Forno
(STUFFED BAKED PEARS)

These baked pears are really delicious. I like them much better than the famous pears Helène, which are nothing more than cooked or canned pears with chocolate sauce. The filling of raisins (which can be soaked in rum for extra flavor— I recommend it) and walnuts makes the pears very tasty and worthy of a formal dinner, served together with Malvasia d'Asti.

6 large pears	*½ cup chopped walnuts*
½ cup raisins	*2 tbsp. sugar*
¼ cup dry white wine	*¼ cup Marsala wine*

Wash and drain pears. Cut in half lengthwise and core. Place on a buttered 11¾″ × 7½″ Pyrex baking pan. Mix raisins—softened for ½ hour in white wine—walnuts, and sugar in a bowl. Pour Marsala over them; stuff into pear halves. Bake at 350° for 15 minutes. Serve either warm or cold.

Pesche Ripiene al Forno con Zabaione
(BAKED STUFFED PEACHES WITH ZABAIONE)

This, my favorite summer dessert, is always very successful. Since it is delicate as well as unusual it will do very well for a formal dinner party. Although the maraschino cherries add a brighter note of color to the gold of the *zabaione*, I prefer the taste of fresh bing cherries, which I cut in two and use for decoration. What is left of the *zabaione* after covering the peaches can be put in a little pitcher and placed on the table if anyone wants more.

8 large freestone peaches   *6 oz. almond macaroons*
¼ cup sugar   *8 maraschino cherries*
1 egg

Cut peaches in halves and remove pits. Scoop out some pulp and put into blender or mixer with sugar and eggs. Add macaroons, finely ground; fill peach halves with mixture. Place on a buttered baking sheet. Bake at 325° for 50 minutes or until filling rises and begins to crack. Let cool; place on a serving dish. Serve covered with *zabaione* (p. 106) and decorated with maraschino cherries cut in half.

Pesche Gelate ai Lamponi
(ICED PEACHES WITH RASPBERRIES)

In spite of the rather lengthy procedure, this is a rather easy dessert to make; even if you take a shortcut and buy the ice cream in a store instead of making it yourself, it will be worthy of the great Italian tradition of frozen desserts. It's very tasty and pretty—all cream colored, golden, and red.

6 *freestone peaches*	1 *tbsp. powdered sugar*
¾ *cup granulated sugar*	1 *qt. plus 1 pt. vanilla*
¼ *cup Kirsch*	*ice cream*
½ *lb. raspberries*	

Place peaches in a pan of boiling water for 2–3 minutes. Drain; peel, cut in half, and remove pits. Place side by side in a deep serving dish. Put 1 qt. of water in a pan; add granulated sugar and let boil until sugar is melted. Pour over peaches; add Kirsch, less 1 tsp. Refrigerate. Wash, drain, and mash raspberries, except for a dozen to be used for decoration. Add powdered sugar and the 1 tsp. Kirsch; mix well. Drain peaches and stuff with raspberry mixture.

Line a 2-qt. mold with 1 qt. vanilla ice cream. Place a few peaches on the bottom and cover with rest of ice cream. Alternate peaches and ice cream, ending with ice cream. Cover with waxed paper and freeze 2–3 hours. Unmold and serve immediately. (To unmold it more easily, place for a second in a pan of hot water.) Garnish with rest of raspberries.

Composto di Frutta e Crema
(FRUIT AND CREAM COMPOTE)

Quite often I discover that I have some fruit in the house which is rapidly becoming overripe. When this happened to me once I thought I would do something with it different from the usual compote—something more like the American chiffon pie. The advantage of this recipe is that you can use any kind of fruit you have on hand, all mixed together, which gives a richer and fresher fruity taste to the dessert. Serve it to your family and friends for dinner and you can be sure they will like it.

2 *oranges*	1 *small can pitted cherries*
4 *apricots*	4 *tbsp. sugar*
2 *peaches*	2 *eggs, separated*
2 *pears or any other fruit in*	1 *cup milk*
season	1 *tbsp. flour*
	½ *tsp. cream of tartar*

Wash oranges; slice finely. Wash rest of fruit and chop into medium size pieces. Place all fruit in a pan with cherries, their juice, and 1 tbsp. sugar. Cook until soft. Remove from heat and let cool. Make a custard with egg yolks, 2 tbsp. sugar, milk, and flour. Beat egg whites with cream of tartar and 1 tbsp. sugar until stiff. Place fruit compote in a buttered 10″ Pyrex baking pan; cover with custard and meringue. Bake in a hot oven (500°) for 4–5 minutes, until meringue is slightly golden. Serve warm or cold.

Macedonia di Frutta
(ITALIAN FRUIT SALAD)

This is one of the classic Italian desserts which is very easy to make. As in the preceding recipe, you can use any kind of fruit—the more the better. Plain tea cookies or *amaretti* (almond macaroons, p. 39) should accompany it. It is particularly well suited for a dinner where rich food is served. Any muscatel wine will go well with it.

2 apples	1 bunch seedless grapes
2 pears	1 cup diced cantaloupe
2 peaches	1 cup diced watermelon
4 apricots	1 banana
2 slices pineapple	½ cup sugar
1 cup strawberries or raspberries	½ cup Cointreau

Peel, core, and chop apples and pears. Wash and drain peaches and apricots; remove pits and cut into small pieces. Dice pineapple. Wash and drain strawberries and grapes. Add diced cantaloupe and watermelon. Peel and slice banana. Put fruit in a large glass or china bowl; add sugar and Cointreau. Mix well and put in refrigerator for 1–2 hours. Serve in sherbet glasses.

Note: For more festive occasions, Asti Spumante, an Italian sweet sparkling wine, can be used instead of Cointreau.

Ices, Ice Cream, and Spumoni

Ices and Ice Creams: A Note

According to reliable sources, the Chinese invented ices and taught Indians how to make them. From India this art passed on to Persia and Arabia, and the Arabs must have brought it to Italy via Sicily. The Greeks, Romans, and the Jews of Palestine also used to make ices—chilling juices and wine or making a concoction of milk, cream, and snow. Very likely the first Italian fruit ice was the one made at the court of the Roman Emperor Nero. It consisted of snow flavored with honey, juice, and fruit pulp. In wintertime snow and ice were carried on large carts from the mountains and buried underground, covered with straw. Mounds of soil massed on top of them would keep them frozen until summer. The same procedure was followed in later centuries, only then the snow was stored in cellars, which also served as refrigerators for perishable goods. The first and most famous ice cream makers were Sicilians and Neapolitans, although the first recipe for a frozen dessert with milk, similar to sherbet, was brought to Venice by Marco Polo on his return from China; a Genoese, Giovanni Bosio, was the first to sell ice cream in America. In the 16th century ices and sherbets were already quite popular in Italy and also in Spain at the court of Philip II, whose son Don Carlos was said to consume enormous amounts of them. In 1533 Caterina de Medici brought them to Paris with her own chefs when, at the age of 14, she married the Duke of Orléans, later Henri II. But the one who gave international fame to ices and sherbets was a destitute young Sicilian nobleman, Procopio dei Coltelli. He went to Paris in 1662, and a few years later opened a café modeled after the Venetian coffee shop Florian, where together with typical Sicilian pastry and liqueurs he sold ices and sherbets. Pretty soon everybody in Paris knew the Café Procope and extolled its marvelous frozen desserts. The forefather of modern ice cream was another Italian, the famous Tortoni, owner of the café of the same name, which had a great popularity in Paris at the end of the 18th century. From Italy ice creams came to America, and then went back to Italy in the 20th century, mass produced, chemically treated, and artificially colored. It is difficult now even there to find ice cream parlors, coffee houses, or restaurants where ice cream has still the pristine lightness and genuine flavor. But there are still a few ice cream makers left worthy of the old tradition. In Venice our favorite has always been Titta's on the Lido. My father used to take us there for some special treat every Sunday afternoon when we were children. Years later he would take my children to Titta's on our summer visits to Venice. Some of the ices and ice creams of which I am giving you the recipes have been inspired by Titta's masterpieces, some I owe to one of my father's orderlies, who had been a pastry chef on an admiral's ship, and the rest are my own creations.

Granita di Fragole
(STRAWBERRY GRANITA)

In the old times water ices and sherbets like these were served halfway between main courses during banquets as refreshers or to revive the appetite. Today, the *granita* is the only one among the frozen desserts which still keeps its genuine character in every part of Italy. It does not require any special freezing procedure and can be made on the spur of the moment in no time at all. It is very cooling and ideal for a summer afternoon or evening.

2 *lb. strawberries*	2 *cups water*
½ *lemon*	1½ *cups sugar*

Wash and drain strawberries; mash well. Place in a bowl and pour juice of lemon over. Set aside. Boil water with sugar until sugar is melted; remove from heat and let cool. Add to strawberries. Mix well and strain. Pour into ice trays and freeze to semisolid mush, without stirring, 1–2 hours. Serve in tall glasses.

Granita di Limone
(LEMON GRANITA)

2 *cups water*	2 *lemons*
1 *cup sugar*	1 *lemon peel*

Boil water with sugar until sugar is melted. Remove from heat and let cool. Add juice of two lemons plus one peel.

Strain and freeze as for strawberry *granita* and serve in tall glasses.

Granita di Caffè
(COFFEE GRANITA)

2 cups water   4 cups coffee
1¾ cups sugar   ½ cup whipping cream

Boil water with sugar until sugar is melted. Remove from heat and let cool. Add cold coffee. Freeze as for other *granite* and pour in tall glasses. Top each serving with 1 tbsp. whipped cream.

Gelato di Crema alla Vaniglia
(VANILLA ICE CREAM)

5 egg yolks   2 cups milk
12 tbsp. sugar   1 tsp. vanilla extract

Beat egg yolks and sugar well in double boiler; add milk and vanilla. Cook slowly, continuing mixing, until slightly thickened. Remove from heat and let cool. Put into freezer trays and freeze for about 3 hours.

Note: This is the basis for most ice creams. Milk can be partly replaced by whipping cream, to be added during freezing process. This addition makes the ice cream richer and softer.

Gelato di Crema al Limone
(LEMON-FLAVORED VANILLA ICE CREAM)

3 egg yolks	1 cup water
1 cup sugar	1 lemon peel
1 cup milk	

Make a custard following the procedure as in previous basic recipe, but eliminate vanilla and add lemon peel. Remove peel when cool; freeze for about 3 hours, stirring once or twice.

Gelato di Caffè
(COFFEE ICE CREAM)

5 egg yolks	1½ cups milk
1 cup sugar	½ cup strong coffee

Make a custard following the same procedure as in recipe on p. 84, except eliminate vanilla and add coffee; freeze for about 3 hours, stirring once. Half a cup of whipping cream can be substituted for ½ cup of milk, to be added before freezing.

Gelato di Cioccolata
(CHOCOLATE ICE CREAM)

Follow recipe on p. 84, except omit vanilla and add ¾ cup powdered chocolate. With this ice cream you can make a *Bomba al cioccolato* (Chocolate Dome-shaped Ice Cream): Line a chilled 1-qt. round mold with chocolate ice cream, leaving an empty space inside which will be filled with 1 pt. whipped cream. Cover and freeze until firm, about 3 hours. To serve, place for a second or two under hot water and turn out on a serving dish.

Gelato di Banane
(BANANA ICE CREAM)

Follow recipe on p. 84, except omit vanilla and add 1 cup mashed bananas and 1 tsp. lemon juice.

Gelato di Mandorle, Noci, o Nocciole
(ALMOND, WALNUT, OR HAZELNUT ICE CREAM)

Follow recipe on p. 84, except omit vanilla and add ½ cup finely ground toasted almonds or nuts. Leave a few nuts whole for decoration.

Gelato di Pistacchio
(PISTACHIO ICE CREAM)

Follow recipe on p. 84, except omit vanilla and add ½ cup pistachio nuts, chopped, and a little green food coloring.

Gelato di Zabaione
(ZABAIONE ICE CREAM)

Follow recipe on p. 84, except omit vanilla and add ¼ cup Marsala wine when ice cream is half frozen.

Gelati di Frutta
(FRUIT ICES)

Fruit ices are made the same way as the *granite*, but they have a smoother texture because of a higher sugar content and longer freezing time.

Basic recipe:
   1 lb. fruit   *4 cups water*
   2 cups sugar

Cook and strain fruit. Bring sugar and water to boil and add fruit. Let cool; put into freezer trays. Freeze until firm (about 3 hours), stirring two or three times. When it is frozen until firm, you may want to turn it out into a chilled bowl and beat with a rotary beater until fluffy, return to freezer and freeze again until firm.

For *Pineapple Ice* I experimented, adding the juice of a lemon to pineapple juice and fruit. It turned out to be the most delicious pineapple ice—light as freshly fallen snow— with just a faint flavor of lemon. Here is the recipe:

> 1½ cups water
> ½ cup unsweetened
>   pineapple juice
> juice of a lemon
>
> 1⅓ cups sugar
> 4 slices canned pineapple,
>   chopped

In order to give it an even smoother texture I used my electric ice cream maker. I left it in for 25 minutes, and then stored it in the freezer for about 3 hours in plastic containers. The same can be done for any kind of fruit ices and ice creams.

For *Lemon Ice*, add the juice of a lemon (about ¼ cup) and 1 egg white beaten stiff to the 2 cups sugar and 4 cups water.

For *Strawberry Ice*, add 1 lb. fresh or frozen strawberries, put through a sieve or pureed in an electric blender, to lemon ice. Mix well; pour into ice tray and freeze. The same can be done for RASPBERRY ICE. Otherwise you can use the basic recipe for fruit ices, substituting the juice of a lemon for ½ cup of water, and adding 1 egg white beaten stiff.

For *Grapefruit Ice*, use 1 cup water, 1¾ cups grapefruit juice, and ¼ cup lemon juice.

For *Orange Ice*, instead of 2 cups water, use 1½ cups fresh orange juice and ½ cup lemon juice. Add the grated peel of 1 orange (optional) and 1 egg white beaten stiff.

Semi-Freddo alla Frutta
(FRUIT "SEMI-FREDDO")

This is a very easy, sure-fire dessert. Although it is a little rich, it can also be served after rather substantial dinner courses together with Asti Spumante.

2 *bananas*	1 *cup candied cherries*
1 *pear*	½ *cup Cointreau*
1 *peach*	2 *cups whipping cream*
1 *slice pineapple*	¾ *cup powdered sugar*

Peel bananas, pear, and peach. Cut, with pineapple, into small pieces. Place in a bowl with cherries and pour Cointreau diluted in water over fruit. Let stand for 2–3 hours in refrigerator. Whip cream; add powdered sugar and fruit, well drained. Mix lightly. Pour into a 2-qt. mold; refrigerate for 3–4 hours. Unmold and serve immediately. (To unmold more easily place in a pan of hot water for a second.)

Spumone
(SPUMONI)

This is the first of a variety of typical Italian desserts of which there are as many versions as pastry chefs. This recipe and the following ones are my own versions. In an American cookbook I found a recipe for *spumone* with commercially made ice cream and homemade mousse. Using ice cream is a shortcut, but I do not recommend it to anyone who wants to make a genuine Italian *spumone*. As its name, which comes from *spuma* ("foam") indicates, its texture must be very light, almost foamy. It is a very elaborate and elegant dessert which is well suited for a formal dinner together with Verdicchio di Jesi.

First mixture:
5 *egg yolks*	3 *cups milk*
1 *cup sugar*	½ *tsp. vanilla*
2 *tbsp. cornstarch*	

Second mixture:
1½ *cups whipping cream*	2 *tbsp. chopped candied*
½ *cup sugar*	*orange peel*
10 *maraschino cherries*	

Put egg yolks, sugar, and cornstarch in double boiler; beat until creamy. Add milk and vanilla a little at a time; cook slowly until thickened, continuing stirring. Remove from heat, cool, and place in refrigerator tray in freezer compartment for about 2 hours.

To prepare second mixture, whip cream until stiff; add sugar, chopped-up cherries, and orange peel. Place in refrigerator.

Remove first mixture from tray and line a *spumone* mold (or 1-qt. jelly mold) with it. Top with second mixture. Cover tightly with waxed paper and freeze for 2 hours. To unmold dip *spumone* for a second in a pan of hot water.

Spumone al Cioccolato
(CHOCOLATE SPUMONI)

5 *egg yolks*	3 *squares semisweet baking*
1 *cup sugar*	*chocolate*
2 *tbsp. cornstarch*	2 *cups whipping cream*
3 *cups milk*	

Make a thick custard with egg yolks, sugar, cornstarch, and milk as in recipe for *spumone*. Melt chocolate in a pan at low heat, adding a little water. Pour into custard; mix well and let stand in freezer for 2 hours. Remove from tray; add whipped cream and put into *spumone* mold (or 1-qt. jelly mold). Cover and freeze for 2 hours.

Spumone al Caffè
(COFFEE SPUMONI)

Follow recipe for *spumone al cioccolato*, except add 3 tbsp. powdered instant coffee to custard instead of chocolate.

Spumone allo Zabaione
(ZABAIONE SPUMONI)

This is possibly the most delicious *spumone* of all, and will be enthusiastically welcomed by all those who love zabaione.

Make zabaione, following the recipe on p. 106. Let cool; add 2 cups cream, well whipped. Pour into *spumone* mold (or 1-qt. jelly mold). Cover with waxed paper and freeze for 2 hours.

Spumone di Pere
(PEAR SPUMONI)

2 lb. pears
½ cup sugar
1 glass dry white wine

⅓ cup Cointreau
1½ cups whipping cream
1 tbsp. butter

Wash and peel pears; cut in halves, remove cores, and slice finely. Put in a pan with sugar and wine; cook until dry, stirring occasionally. Remove from heat and put through a sieve into a bowl. Add Cointreau; mix well and let cool. Whip cream; fold into pear mixture and pour into well-buttered pudding mold. Cover with waxed paper and refrigerate for at least 3 hours.

Budino Gelato di Caffè Adriana
(ADRIANA'S COFFEE ICE PUDDING)

My friend Adriana gave me the recipe for this dessert many years ago. It is very delicate and easy to make. I remember having eaten it at her house with nut cookies or pastry for dinner or tea.

4 eggs
½ cup sugar
¾ cup strong coffee

1 pack gelatine
2 cups whipping cream

Beat eggs and sugar in double boiler until creamy. Add coffee a little at a time and cook slowly, continuing mixing until thickened. Remove from heat and whip well. Add gelatine dissolved in a little water. Let cool. Fold in whipped cream and put into 1-qt. mold, tightly covered with waxed paper. Refrigerate for 3–4 hours.

Creams, Puddings, Mousses, and Soufflés

Crema Pasticcera
(PASTRY CREAM)

This type of pastry cream, and its variations which follow, are used as filling for cakes or, as in the case of lemon cream, in combination with fresh fruit peeled and chopped, and served chilled in sherbet glasses. Two tablespoons of Marsala wine added to pastry cream will give it a delicious zabaione taste.

2 egg yolks	*1 tbsp. flour*
2 tbsp. sugar	*1½ cups milk*

Place egg yolks, sugar, and flour in a double boiler. Beat until creamy; add milk a little at a time. Cook at low heat,

97

continuing mixing until it thickens. It must not boil. Remove from heat and let cool.

Variations:

I—*Crema al cioccolato*/Chocolate Cream. Add ¼ cup melted baking chocolate to the above recipe.

II—*Crema al limone*/Lemon Cream. Add a lemon peel to the pastry cream while it cooks. The peel is removed before custard is set aside to cool.

III—*Crema fritta*/Fried Cream. This is made with lemon cream, substituting 1 whole egg for 1 yolk and using 3 cups flour and 1 cup milk together with the 2 tbsp. sugar. Follow the same procedure as for pastry cream. When cream is pretty thick, add one pinch salt; mix well and pour onto moistened marble surface or large serving dish. Let cool and cut into 2″ × 2″ squares. Flour lightly; dip in beaten egg and bread crumbs. Deep fry in vegetable shortening until golden brown; serve warm sprinkled with powdered sugar. In many good Italian restaurants *crema fritta* is served with fine cuts of meat or fish.

Crema d'Arancio
(ORANGE CREAM)

This orange cream and the other creams, puddings, mousses, and soufflés in this chapter are very delicate and light desserts, well suited for formal dinners. The one exception, perhaps, is the ricotta pudding, which is the plainest of them all and, although excellent, should be served for family or informal dinners. Any muscatel wine will be perfect with them.

4 tbsp. gelatine	grated rind of 1 orange
1½ cups milk	¼ cup Cointreau
½ cup sugar	2 cups whipping cream

Dilute gelatine with some water. Put milk, sugar, and orange rind in double boiler and cook for about 10 minutes, mixing well. Add gelatine; mix and remove from heat. Add Cointreau and let cool. Fold in whipped cream; pour into mold or sherbet glasses. Let stand a few hours in refrigerator. Serve chilled.

Crema di Caffè
(COFFEE CREAM)

5 *egg yolks*	1 *tbsp. strong coffee*
¾ *cup sugar*	¼ *cup granulated gelatine*
1 *tsp. vanilla extract*	1 *cup whipping cream*
1 *cup milk*	

Beat yolks with sugar and vanilla until creamy. Add milk, coffee, gelatine diluted in some water and strained, and whipped cream. Pour into single cups or sherbet glasses; leave for 2–3 hours in refrigerator.

Crema di Castagne
(CHESTNUT CREAM)

2 *lb. chestnuts*	1 *cup powdered sugar*
2 *cups milk*	1 *cup whipping cream*

Peel chestnuts; cover with water and boil for about 15 minutes. Drain; remove inner skin. Mash and mix with milk. Cook for about 35 minutes or until very soft. Remove from heat and add sugar. Mix well; put through a food mill. The puree thus obtained will look rather like a heap of very thin noodles. Do not stir or beat the puree, but pile it loosely on a serving dish in a cone-shaped mound. Chill and serve covered with whipped cream.

Crema Diplomatica
(DIPLOMATIC CREAM)

4 squares baking chocolate	½ cup whipping cream
4 eggs, separated	6 candied cherries
1¼ cups powdered sugar	1 doz. pistachio nuts

Melt chocolate in double boiler; add 4 tbsp. water and mix well. Remove from heat. When cool, add egg yolks well beaten with sugar, less 1 tsp., and stiffly beaten egg whites. Pour into 1-qt. mold without filling it completely; freeze for 30 minutes. Serve decorated with whipped cream, 1 tsp. powdered sugar, candied cherry halves, and pistachio nuts.

Budino di Castagne
(CHESTNUT PUDDING)

2½ lb. chestnuts	1 tsp. vanilla extract
¾ cup butter	1 tsp. baking powder
4 eggs, separated	1 tbsp. bread crumbs
1¼ cups sugar	½ cup whipping cream

Peel chestnuts; cover with water and boil for about 15 minutes. Drain; remove inner skins and put through a sieve into a large bowl. Melt butter. Beat egg yolks well with sugar and vanilla. Add butter, egg yolks, and baking powder to chestnuts. Fold in stiffly beaten egg whites; pour mixture into a fluted pudding mold, well greased and sprinkled with bread crumbs. Bake at 325° for about 1 hour. Cool, turn out on a plate, and serve with whipped cream.

Budino di Cioccolata I
(CHOCOLATE PUDDING I)

3 *cups milk*
3 *squares baking chocolate,*
    grated
½ *cup sugar*

1 *cup ladyfingers or*
    shortcake crumbs
3 *eggs*
2 *tsp. caramelized sugar*

Put milk in double boiler with chocolate; when mixture is about to boil add sugar and crumbs. Cook for 20 minutes; strain. Let cool and add to well-beaten eggs. Pour some caramelized sugar into the bottom of a pudding mold, then add pudding mixture; set the mold in a pan of hot water. Bake at 325° for 40–45 minutes or until a knife inserted in pudding comes out clean. Serve chilled.

Note: To make caramelized sugar, follow instructions in note on p. 51.

Budino di Cioccolata II
(CHOCOLATE PUDDING II)

5½ *cups milk*
4 *squares baking chocolate*
6 *eggs*

¾ *cup sugar*
¾ *cup macaroon crumbs*
½ *cup whipping cream*

Heat milk and chocolate in double boiler until chocolate is melted, continuing mixing. Remove from heat; add eggs and sugar beaten together. Continue mixing; cook until thickened. Remove from heat; add macaroon crumbs and beat well. Pour into greased pudding mold and set in refrigerator for a few hours before turning out on a serving dish. Garnish with whipped cream.

Budino Corona di Banane
(BANANA RING PUDDING)

This is a particularly attractive and delicious dessert. The blending of the delicate tastes of the almonds and the bananas is just as pleasant as the combination of the colors of the fruit decorating it.

1 cup blanched almonds　*3 tbsp. butter*
½ cup sugar　*grated rind of ½ lemon*
1 tsp. vanilla　*2 egg yolks*
4 cups milk　*1 banana*
¾ cup flour　*½ doz. candied cherries*

Grind almonds. Put sugar, vanilla, and milk, less 5 tbsp., into double boiler and bring to boil. Mix flour with rest of milk and add to boiling mixture. Mix well; let boil for 5 minutes. Remove from heat; add butter, lemon, and almonds. When mixture is cool, add egg yolks one at a time and beat well. Moisten the inside of an angel-food cake pan or bundt pan with water; pour mixture into pan and freeze for 2 hours. Place pudding upside down on a serving dish. Decorate with banana slices and cherry halves.

Budino di Farina di Riso
(RICE FLOUR PUDDING)

3½ cups milk
1 cup rice flour
½ cup sugar
1 tbsp. butter

pinch of salt
5 eggs
1 tsp. vanilla extract

Put 3 cups milk in double boiler; when boiling, add flour diluted in the rest of milk. Mix well; add sugar, butter, and salt. Remove from heat and let cool. Add well-beaten eggs and vanilla. Pour into well-greased and floured 2-qt. pudding mold. Bake at 325° for about 40 minutes.

Budino di Mandorle
(ALMOND PUDDING)

½ cup blanched almonds
3 cups milk
½ cup sugar
1 cup ladyfingers or
    shortcake crumbs

3 eggs
2 tsp. caramelized sugar
½ cup whipping cream
    (optional)

Toast and grind almonds. Put milk in double boiler with sugar, almonds, and crumbs; cook for about 10 minutes, mixing well. Remove from heat; strain. When cool add well-beaten eggs. Pour 2 tsp. caramelized sugar into the bottom of a pudding mold set in a pan of hot water; add mixture. Bake at 325° for 40–45 minutes or until a knife inserted in pudding comes out clean. Serve chilled and, if you like, with whipped cream.

Note: To make caramelized sugar, follow instructions in note on p. 51.

Budino di Ricotta
(RICOTTA PUDDING) Good ?

This is a very popular dessert in central and southern Italy. This is my own version, and even if you change the measurements of the ingredients a little, it will come out well just the same. Health food fans can substitute brown sugar for the white sugar. It is a filling but not fattening dessert, which could even be used as a main course, after a salad or soup, for a light supper.

1½ lb. ricotta	*1 tbsp. flour*
½ cup sugar	*¼ cup raisins*
4 eggs, separated	*grated rind of 1 lemon*

Mix ricotta with sugar, egg yolks, flour, floured raisins, and lemon rind. Fold in egg whites beaten stiff; pour mixture into a greased and floured pudding mold. Bake at 350° for about 50 minutes. Let cool before turning out on a serving dish.

Mousse di Cioccolata
(CHOCOLATE MOUSSE)

You may wonder how it is that you find desserts with French names in a book of Italian desserts. Well, we Italians have our own versions of mousses and soufflés and they are just as delicious as the others. This recipe for chocolate mousse was given to me by a friend many years ago, and has always been one of my favorites.

4 squares baking chocolate	*1 tsp. gelatine*
2 cups milk	*1 egg, separated*
1½ cups sugar	*1 pt. whipping cream*

Melt chocolate in double boiler with milk, 1 cup sugar, and gelatine dissolved in a little water. Cook slowly and bring to boil. Remove from heat and cool. Add egg yolk beaten with rest of sugar until creamy; pour into a bowl. Refrigerate until well chilled.

Beat egg white stiff and whip cream. Fold into chocolate mixture; pour into large mold or sherbet glasses. Freeze 3–4 hours for mold, 2 hours for glasses.

Mousse di Pesche o Altra Frutta di Stagione
(PEACH OR OTHER FRUIT MOUSSE)

1 lb. freestone peaches	*1 tsp. gelatine*
¾ cup sugar	*1 pt. whipping cream*

Wash and drain peaches. Cut in half and remove pits. Put into blender or through a sieve until well mashed. Place in bowl with sugar and gelatine dissolved in a little water. Refrigerate. When well chilled, fold in whipped cream and pour into large mold or sherbet glasses. Freeze 3–4 hours for mold, 2 hours for glasses.

Note: Any other fruit in season in a quantity large enough to get 1 cup mashed pulp can be substituted for peaches.

Zabaione
(ZABAIONE)

This Marsala wine sauce is certainly the most famous Italian dessert. There are many versions of it. An American lady we know served it to us for dinner some time ago, and since she wanted to have it ready well in advance she cheated a little and added whipped cream to it. The typical zabaione flavor was still there, but the texture was slightly changed. Better leave the whipped cream out. Zabaione is also excellent with fresh fruit chopped up, or even with canned peaches or pears. I advise you to pour it on at the last minute, though, after the fruit is well chilled, in order to avoid the zabaione's being diluted by the moistness left in the fruit, which will happen even when the fruit is well drained.

6 *egg yolks*   1 *cup Marsala wine*
¾ *cup powdered sugar*

Beat egg yolks and sugar until creamy in double boiler; add Marsala. Cook at low heat, continuing beating until thickened. Remove from heat; keep beating until lukewarm. Pour into sherbet glasses. Serve as is or ice cold, or poured over fresh or canned peaches, pears, or grapes.

Zuppa di Ciliege
(CHERRY CAKE)

Zuppa actually means "soup," but when this term is used for a dessert, it always means a moist sponge cake to which either fruit or custard has been added. This is a particularly good one, both tasty and pretty on account of its decoration of cherries and whipped cream, making it very suitable for an elegant dinner. Serve it with Malvasia d'Asti, which has the same ruby color as the cherries.

¾ *lb. pan di Spagna or pound cake*	½ *lb. canned pitted black cherries*
¼ *cup rum or Kirsch*	½ *pt. whipping cream*

Line a wet pudding mold with *pan di Spagna* or pound cake, sliced and moistened with rum or Kirsch diluted with a little water. Alternate layers of cherries and cake until mold is full, ending with cake. Refrigerate for a few hours. Turn out on serving dish and decorate with cherries and whipped cream.

Zuppa di Ricotta
(RICOTTA CAKE)

½ *lb. ricotta*	¼ *cup rum or Cointreau*
¼ *cup powdered sugar*	*apricot or peach preserves*
2 *doz. ladyfingers*	*to taste*

Mix ricotta well with sugar. Line a greased 2-qt. pudding mold with ladyfingers; moisten them with rum or Cointreau diluted with a little water. Put ricotta at the bottom of mold and alternate layers of moistened ladyfingers, preserves, and ricotta until mold is full, ending with layer of ladyfingers. Keep in refrigerator for a few hours before turning out on serving dish.

Zuppa Inglese Roberta
(ROBERTA'S ITALIAN RUM CAKE)

This is another famous Italian dessert bearing the incongruous name of "English Soup," maybe because it is similar to the English trifle. The simplest version of *zuppa inglese* is without meringue and has alternating layers of sliced *pan di Spagna* or ladyfingers and custard. It is served well chilled. I owe the recipe above to my friend Roberta Albori, a charming Italian lady living in Los Angeles, who is also a great cook.

Dough:
See recipe for *pan de Spagna,*
p. 5.

Filling and meringue:
⅓ *cup rum (or 1 tsp. vodka*   *1 tbsp. flour*
    and 1 tsp. extract)   *1½ cups milk*
3 eggs, separated   *½ tsp. cream of tartar*
3 tbsp. sugar

Slice *pan di Spagna* vertically and line a round and deep Pyrex baking pan with overlapping slices. Moisten slices with rum (or vodka and rum extract) diluted with a little water. Make a custard with egg yolks, 2 tbsp. sugar, flour, and milk; pour into the pan. Aside, make a meringue with egg whites, cream of tartar, and the remaining sugar; pour onto custard. Bake at 300° for 15–20 minutes. Serve cold.

Soufflé di Castagne
(CHESTNUT SOUFFLÉ)

This is a rather unusual dessert, well worth trying when chestnuts are in season and you want to offer your guests something they most likely have never had before. It is more moist than other soufflés, and you don't have to worry so much about the soufflé losing its puffy airiness. One rule to observe while making soufflés is never to open the oven door to peek while they are cooking. If you are in doubt, it is better to leave them 5 minutes longer, but if you absolutely must look, wait until the soufflé has been in the oven for 35 minutes. It is also better to always serve them in the same dish you have baked them in—and immediately after taking them out of the oven.

1½ lb. chestnuts	½ cup sugar
2 cups milk	1 pint whipping cream
1 tsp. vanilla extract	(optional)
2 tbsp. butter	1 tbsp. powdered sugar
5 eggs, separated	(optional)

Peel chestnuts, cover with water and boil for about 5 minutes. Drain; remove inner skin and cook with milk until soft. Drain; put through a sieve into a bowl. Add vanilla, melted butter, and egg yolks beaten well with sugar. Fold in stiffly beaten egg whites and pour whole mixture into a greased and floured 2-qt. Pyrex or porcelain soufflé dish. Bake at 325° for about 40 minutes or until a knife inserted in soufflé comes out clean. Serve warm with whipped cream or sprinkled with powdered sugar.

Soufflé di Cioccolata
(CHOCOLATE SOUFFLÉ)

The very first time I tried this recipe, which I had had for quite awhile, was when we had a very special dinner guest, the art patron and world traveler Joseph H. Hirshhorn. The news that he had requested a chocolate soufflé for dessert reached me the very day of our dinner, so I had no time to try out the recipe before. The soufflé came out all right, and I had many compliments, but I was worried until the last minute!

2 tbsp. butter	5 eggs, separated
3 squares baking chocolate	½ cup sugar
2 tbsp. flour	1 tbsp. rum
2 cups milk	

Melt butter and chocolate in double boiler; add flour. Mix well; pour in milk. Keep mixing and cook until thickened. Remove from heat and let cool. Add yolks beaten with sugar and rum. Fold in stiffly beaten egg whites; pour into 3-qt. Pyrex or porcelain soufflé dish, well greased and floured. Bake at 325° for about 40 minutes.

Soufflé di Farina Gialla
(CORN FLOUR SOUFFLÉ)

I don't know whether anyone would want to take the trouble of making a soufflé with something as plain and rustic as yellow corn flour, but I thought of adding it to my selection as a curiosity. I got the idea for this recipe in Abruzzi, where, of course, it is not called a soufflé, but has some indigenous name I don't remember. It is actually a glamorized version of corn bread, but much lighter and tastier.

2 tbsp. butter	2 cups milk
pinch of salt	½ cup sugar
¾ cup yellow corn flour	6 eggs, separated

Place butter, salt, and flour in double boiler; mix well. Add milk and 1 tbsp. sugar. Cook until thick; remove from heat and let cool. Add egg yolks beaten with rest of sugar; mix well. Fold in stiffly beaten egg whites; pour into 3-qt. Pyrex or porcelain soufflé dish, well greased and floured. Bake at 325° for about 45 minutes.

Soufflé Grand Marnier
(GRAND MARNIER SOUFFLÉ)

I wanted to end this short selection of Italian soufflés with the most elegant of them all. It is really a marvelous dessert, which will always be enthusiastically welcomed by your guests. I suggest serving it with some special wine, such as Moscato d'Asti Spumante.

2 cups milk	4 tbsp. Grand Marnier
¾ cup sugar	6 eggs, separated
5 tbsp. butter	1 dozen ladyfingers
½ cup flour	

Put 1½ cups milk, ¼ cup sugar, and butter in double boiler. Mix flour with remaining milk and add to mixture.

Cook until thickened and about to boil; remove from heat and add 2 tbsp. Grand Marnier. Let cool. Add egg yolks well beaten with rest of sugar; fold in stiffly beaten egg whites. Grease and flour a 3-qt. Pyrex or porcelain soufflé dish and pour in ⅓ of mixture. Place a layer of ladyfingers moistened with rest of Grand Marnier on top, then some more mixture and ladyfingers, ending with mixture. Bake at 325° for about 40 minutes.

Regional Specialties

Babà al Rum alla Genovese
(RUM CAKE GENOVESE STYLE)

This is a famous dessert which is on the menus of the best Italian restaurants. I would not recommend it for dinner, though, because no matter how light the dough comes out, it is still a little too heavy to be served after a substantial main course. It is well suited, instead, for a buffet or afternoon coffee or tea.

1 tbsp. yeast	*5 tbsp. sugar*
1¾ cups flour	*pinch of salt*
4 eggs	*½ cup rum*
½ cup butter	

Dissolve yeast in lukewarm water in a bowl and add 1 cup flour. Mix well; cover and let rise until double in size (about 20 minutes). Add rest of flour, eggs, butter, 2 tbsp. sugar, and salt. Knead well until dough is smooth and elastic. Place dough in well-buttered 1½-qt. tubular fluted pudding mold. Put in warm place and let rise about 1½ hours. (The dough should reach the top of the pan.) Bake at 400° for 20 minutes. A few minutes before cake is ready, put rest of sugar with ½ cup water in a small pan and bring to boil. Add rum; remove from heat and pour over cake. Serve warm or cold.

Bavarese Lombarda
(BAVARIAN CREAM LOMBARDY STYLE)

This is one of my favorite desserts. It has a delicious creamy texture and very delicate flavor. When well chilled, it can easily be cut in wedges and served with a chocolate or wine sauce. I prefer it plain. Although very rich, it is quite suitable for a formal dinner: just make small servings. It should be served with only a slightly sweet wine, such as Verdicchio di Jesi.

6 eggs	*1½ dozen ladyfingers*
¾ cup butter	*2 jiggers Grand Marnier or*
1½ cup powdered sugar	* Cointreau*
1 tsp. vanilla extract	

Hard boil eggs; mash yolks with butter. Discard egg whites. Put egg yolks through a sieve; add powdered sugar and vanilla. Mix well. Moisten ladyfingers with liqueur diluted with some water; line 2-qt. pudding mold with them. Add egg yolks mixture and cover it with a layer of ladyfingers set side by side. Let stand in refrigerator for 3–4 hours before serving. This can be made the day before.

Biscotti Dorati alla Piacentina
(GOLDEN COOKIES PIACENZA STYLE)

These cookies are very light, good, and easy to make. This recipe was given to me by a friend of my aunt's, who always served them to us for tea.

½ cup butter	3 tsp. baking powder
¾ cup sugar	½ tsp. salt
4 eggs	1 tsp. vanilla extract
4 cups flour	1 egg yolk

Cream butter with sugar and eggs in a large bowl. Add half the flour sifted with baking powder and salt, and vanilla. Remove mixture from bowl and place on a floured board. Add rest of flour and make a soft dough. Roll out flat ¼″ thick. Cut out cookies with your favorite cookie cutter. Brush with egg yolk; place on a greased baking sheet. Bake at 325° for 10 minutes or until golden brown.

Bombole al Forno alla Veneziana
(VENETIAN PASTRY PUFFS)

These *bombole* are unfailingly a great success both with children and adults. They look a little like round sweet rolls, but they are much lighter. My best friend Laura Gatti and

I used to make them in her family chalet on the Alps on rainy days for a whole gang of kids, and we ate them just out of the oven with the jam still boiling hot inside them.

½ oz. dry yeast
1 cup lukewarm milk
4 cups flour
3 tbsp. sugar
3 whole eggs
¼ cup butter

1 tsp. rum extract
1 tsp. lemon extract
1 tsp. vanilla extract
1 tsp. apricot, peach, or
 raspberry jam
1 egg yolk

Dissolve yeast with milk in a mixing bowl; add 1 cup flour, and sugar. Let rise for 2 hours. Mix rest of flour with yeast dough and combine with 3 eggs, butter, and rum, lemon, and vanilla extracts. Roll out dough on a floured board and knead well. Return to bowl; cover and let rise for ½ hour. Take 1 tbsp. of dough and place on board. Flatten it with palm of hand and put 1 tsp. jam on it. Roll into ball. Follow same procedure until all dough has been used. Arrange balls on a greased baking pan and brush with egg yolk. Bake at 325° for about 45 minutes until well puffed and golden brown.

Cannoli alla Siciliana
(SICILIAN CANNOLI)

This is a very famous dessert, of which the Sicilians can quite rightly be proud. A Venetian friend of mine, whose father's family is from Sicily, gave me this recipe and the one following. This one requires some special equipment: *cannoli* tubes, which are metal or bamboo tubes about 7″ long and 1″ in diameter. They can be bought in any gourmet or restaurant supply store in this country, but the first time I made the *cannoli* as a child, my brother and I went to some friends' garden, cut down a couple of bamboo canes, chopped them up in pieces, and made our *cannoli* tubes that way. They are a pretty rich dessert and are better suited for a buffet than for a dinner. On a buffet table they will look very attractive, all golden brown, sprinkled with sugar and with the ricotta and candied fruit filling showing at the two ends. Positively yummy.

Dough:

1¾ cups flour	*1 cup white wine*
¼ cup powdered sugar	*pinch of salt*
1½ tbsp. butter	

Filling:

1 lb. ricotta	*1 tbsp. chopped candied*
1 cup powdered sugar	*orange peel*
1 tbsp. chopped candied	*2 tbsp. grated chocolate*
cherries	*1 jigger Cointreau*

Make a well-kneaded, elastic dough with the flour, sugar, butter, wine, and salt. Roll into ball; set aside for about 1 hour covered with towel. Mix ricotta, ¾ cup sugar and other filling ingredients in a mixing bowl.

Roll out dough ⅛" thick. Cut into oval or round shapes about 5" in diameter and wrap them around *cannoli* tubes. Fry in hot deep fat, a few at a time, until golden brown. Remove tubes and let cool, then stuff with filling. Serve immediately sprinkled with rest of sugar.

Cassata alla Siciliana
(SICILIAN CASSATA)

Like the *cannoli*, the *cassata* is a rich dessert best suited for a buffet party. To my taste, it is a little too sweet, and

I cut down quite a bit on the sugar—to about half of what this recipe calls for. It looks very pretty with its white icing and decoration of candied fruit, and is very colorful when cut up, which can be done when a little dry crust has formed on the top.

Cake:

> 2 cups granulated sugar
> 1½ lb. ricotta
> 1 cup chopped candied fruit
>
> 1 tbsp. chopped semisweet chocolate
> 1 jigger rum
> 1 lb. pan di Spagna or 1 lb. pound cake

Icing:

> 1 egg white
> 1½ cups powdered sugar
>
> 1 tsp. lemon juice
> 1 doz. candied cherries

Put sugar in a small pan with some water and bring to boil. Remove from heat; let cool. Add ricotta, candied fruit, chocolate, and rum; mix well. Cut *pan di Spagna* or cake into 1″ slices and line a round baking dish. Pour in ricotta mixture and cover with rest of *pan di Spagna*. Let stand 2–3 hours in refrigerator.

Turn over on serving dish and cover with icing made with egg white, powdered sugar, and lemon juice, beaten stiff. Decorate with candied cherry halves. Set in refrigerator for ½ hour before serving.

Castagnaccio Fiorentino o Panella Genovese
(FLORENTINE CHESTNUT PIE OR GENOVESE PANELLA)

Nobody knows really where this excellent chestnut dessert originated. All I can say is that it is called *castagnaccio* in most parts of Italy, while in Genoa it takes the name of *panella*. During chestnut season—late fall and winter—one can buy it in every Italian pastry shop and bakery. It is only about 2″ deep, oily at the bottom, mud colored, a little sticky, and, in spite of all this, absolutely delicious, maybe on account of the combination of pine nuts on top and chestnut flour. Unfortunately, most Italian stores in America don't import chestnut flour, probably because it goes stale very soon. But if you have Italian friends or relatives, you could ask them to send you some. The original Tuscan recipe for *castagnaccio* requires a sprinkling of rosemary leaves on top, but I frankly prefer it without.

3 cups chestnut flour	*½ cup raisins*
pinch of salt	*½ cup pine nuts*
2½ tbsp. oil	

Mix chestnut flour well with salt, oil, and enough water to make mixture creamy. Add raisins moistened with water; pour into well-greased 9″ baking pan. Sprinkle pine nuts on top. Bake at 350° for about 45 minutes, or until little cracks have formed on the top.

Cenci, Frappe, o Chiacchiere Napoletane
(NEAPOLITAN FRITTERS)

This is a dessert traditionally made at *Carnevale* (Italian Halloween) in several parts of Italy. Curiously enough, these fritters are common also in the Middle East, where they are eaten with honey poured on top. I saw something very similar to them in San Francisco's Chinatown, also served with honey. They are very light and crisp, and their names come from their shapes—which can be very irregular (*cenci* means "rags"), or can resemble bows and ties (*frappe*)—and from their light consistency (*chiacchiere* means "chatter"). In our teens the pleasure of eating them was enhanced by a game that we used to play: a boy and a girl would put a long strip of fritter in their mouths, one at each end, to see who could eat more of it. . . . As you can imagine, it was actually a kissing game—Italian style.

1½ cups flour	2 tbsp. powdered sugar
pinch salt	1 tbsp. olive oil or
2 tsp. baking powder	vegetable shortening
2 eggs	grated rind of 1 lemon

Sift together flour, salt, and baking powder on a floured board. Beat eggs and 1 tbsp. sugar well. Add eggs, oil, and grated lemon to flour. Knead well until dough is smooth and elastic. Roll into a ball, cover with a towel, and let stand for ½ hour. Roll out very thin and cut into 1″ wide, 4″ long strips. Pinch some strips in middle; tie others in a loose knot. Fry in hot deep vegetable shortening, a few at a time, until puffed and golden brown. Drain well and let cool. Serve sprinkled with rest of sugar.

Cicerchiata
(ITALIAN HONEY CAKE)

My recipe for *cicerchiata* is from Abruzzi, but this type of dessert is very popular throughout southern Italy.

2½ cups flour	1 pt. honey
4 eggs	2 tbsp. granulated sugar
1 tbsp. olive oil or	¼ tsp. cinnamon (optional)
vegetable shortening	

Sift flour over mixing board; add eggs and oil and knead well. Roll dough up in a ball and bounce it on board to test elasticity. Cut into 8 pieces and roll up into little sticks ⅛″ in diameter. Cut into small pieces the size of peanuts. Fry, a few at a time, in deep vegetable shortening until double in size and golden brown. Place in a large bowl. Put honey in a pan and bring to boil. Throw dough puffs in and mix well. Let cook for 3–4 minutes. Place a small wet mixing bowl in the center of a large serving dish and arrange puffs around it. Shape into a ring with help of a wet wooden spoon. Remove bowl and sprinkle ring with granulated sugar and cinnamon. Let cool. The honey will then harden and the ring can be sliced in small pieces like nougat candy.

Note: For Easter, the center of ring can be filled with sugar eggs and decorated with fresh daisies. In Umbria they add slivered blanched almonds on top.

Crostata
(SHORT PASTRY PIE)

The *crostata* is a dessert very popular in southern Italy.

Dough:
  See recipe for pasta frolla,
  p. 3.

Filling:
  Apricot, peach, raspberry,
    or strawberry jam

Make a dough following recipe for *pasta frolla*; divide into two pieces, one slightly larger than the other. Roll out smaller piece on a floured board to a little more than ⅛″ thick and the size of an inverted 8″ or 9″ baking pan. Line greased and floured pan with dough. Spread your favorite jam or preserves on it, just enough to cover dough. (If spread too thick, it will boil over and burn.) Roll out rest of dough and cut with fluted pastry wheel into ½″ wide strips. Lay half the strips across preserves 1″ apart. Lay other half crosswise on them. Fold lower crust edge over pastry strips and seal with one more strip all around. Bake at 325° for about 45 minutes or until golden brown.

Variation: With this same recipe one can also make different types of pastry, such as jam rings and small nut or cream tarts. For jam rings, cut rolled-out dough with round cookie cutter. Place ½ tsp. jam in center of each cookie and cover with a ring-shaped piece of dough so jam will show. Bake jam rings at 325° for about 20 minutes or until golden brown.

Crostoli Trentini
(FRITTERS TRENTO STYLE)

1½ cups flour	2 tbsp. butter
1 tsp. baking powder	1 jigger Grappa (or cognac)
1 egg	1 tbsp. powdered sugar
2 tbsp. sugar	

Follow procedure of recipe for *cenci, frappe, o chiacchiere napoletane*, page 121.

Dolce a Freddo Piemontese
(PIEDMONTESE CAKE)

The taste of this dessert reminds me very much of that of *caffé valdostano*, coffee from the Val d'Aosta, a beautiful valley at the foot of the Cervino (Matterhorn) in the Piedmontese Alps. It is from there that I brought back both recipes, for the coffee and the cake, together with many pleasant memories. In this *dolce a freddo* the blending of coffee and liqueur is very subtle and delectable. It is an easy-to-make and foolproof dessert, which can be served for a formal dinner together with Sciacchetrà delle Cinqueterre.

½ *cup butter*	¼ *cup rum or Cointreau*
½ *cup sugar*	2 *lb. sponge cake, sliced*
1 *egg, separated*	⅓ *cup strong coffee*

Beat butter with sugar until creamy. Add yolk and liqueur; mix well. Beat egg white until stiff; add to mixture. Dip cake slices in coffee and arrange in layers on a plate, alternating them with egg white mixture. Serve well chilled.

Dolce di Cioccolata alla Pavese
(CHOCOLATE CAKE PAVIA STYLE)

Cake:

½ *cup butter*	1½ *cups flour*
1¼ *cups sugar*	1 *tsp. baking soda*
2 *eggs*	1 *tsp. baking powder*
½ *cup cocoa*	½ *tsp. salt*
1 *cup hot coffee*	

Christmas Icing:

2 egg whites	*slices of candied fruit*
1 cup powdered sugar	*red and silver candy balls*

Cream butter with sugar and eggs one by one. Stir cocoa into coffee and pour into butter mixture. Add dry ingredients sifted together. Mix well; pour into a well-greased and floured 9″ baking pan. Bake at 325° for 40 minutes.

Variation: This recipe can be used to make the *Torta albero di Natale* (Christmas Tree Cake). Bake batter in a 31″ × 9″, 2″ deep greased and floured pan. Cut cake in shape of a Christmas tree. Cover with icing made with egg whites and powdered sugar beaten stiff. Decorate with thin slices of candied fruit and little red and silver candy balls.

Dolce Mirella (Trieste)
(MIRELLA'S CAKE TRIESTE STYLE)

This recipe was given to me by my friend and colleague Mirella Fonda-Bonardi during a breathing spell in the course of our academic labors at UCLA. She guarantees that it improves with time, but it is such a good dessert that it has never lasted more than a day either in her family or mine. It somewhat resembles a sweet roll—with a very light, golden crust on the outside and a delicious, juicy fruit and nut filling —and is excellent for afternoon snacks, coffee or tea, and buffet parties.

Dough:

3½ cups flour	*½ cup powdered sugar*
3 tsp. baking powder	*2 eggs*
pinch of salt	*1 tsp. lemon extract*
6 tbsp. butter	*milk as needed*

Filling:

1 cup ground almonds or
    walnuts
1 cup bread crumbs
    browned in 2 tbsp.
    butter
¼ cup sugar
½ cup grated chocolate

⅓ cup raisins
⅓ cup candied fruit
1 tsp. vanilla
1 tsp. rum extract
grated rind of ½ lemon
1 egg yolk

Sift flour on a board with baking powder and salt; cut in butter. Add sugar, eggs, and lemon extract; mix with a knife, using 2 or 3 tbsp. milk to make a soft dough. Knead lightly; roll out flat about ⅓″ thick on a rectangular sheet of waxed paper.

Combine filling ingredients in a large bowl and spread it on top of the dough; roll it up and brush with egg yolk. Bake at 325° for about 40 minutes.

Dolce Moca alla Ferrarese
(MOCHA CAKE FERRARA STYLE)

This is a very easy, delicate-tasting cake which one can prepare a day ahead. Don't worry about those raw eggs: they are very healthful, and nobody will notice that they are not cooked. This is a dessert similar to the *bavarese lombarda* (p. 116) and also suitable for a formal dinner together with Lambrusco. It was often made in my mother's family, as was the *dolce di riso alla mantovana* that follows this recipe.

¾ cup butter
½ cup sugar
4 eggs
1 tbsp. cognac
½ cup strong coffee
1 lb. ladyfingers

1 cup Marsala wine or
    sweet sherry
½ pint whipping cream
    (optional)
candied fruit (optional)

Cream butter with sugar; add eggs, cognac, and coffee. Grease pudding mold and line with ladyfingers moistened with Marsala or sherry. Pour mixture into mold and chill for a few hours. Before serving, dip for a second in a pan of boiling water and turn upside down onto a plate. Cake can be decorated with whipped cream and candied fruit.

Dolce di Riso alla Mantovana
(RICE CAKE MANTOVA STYLE)

If your children get tired of hamburgers or hot dogs, and you get tired of cooking the same things, try a light supper of rice cake and fresh fruit once. I bet everybody will love it, especially if it is a warm summer evening. This is a very good cake for snacks or picnics also. In a more sophisticated version from the Emilia region—famous for its superb cooking— chopped candied fruit is added to it, the surface is pricked with a skewer, and Maraschino liqueur is poured on top.

1 cup rice	*⅓ cup raisins*
2 cups milk	*⅓ cup butter*
½ cup water	*grated rind of 1 lemon*
½ cup sugar	*3 eggs*

Cook rice in milk and water with sugar and raisins. Let cool; add butter, lemon rind, and eggs. Mix well and pour into a greased and floured 2-qt. Pyrex baking dish. Bake at 325° for 40 minutes until firm with a golden crust.

Fritole Veneziane
(VENETIAN FRITTERS)

These fritters may not be very light and refined, but they are excellent. Just the thought of them evokes for me and all expatriate Venetians the gay confusion and noise of Carnival time in Venice and the all-night festivities in the squatty lagoon rowboats—each one decorated with garlands of vines and Chinese balloons, gently swaying on the dark water under a black sky lit by sudden, starlike outbursts of fireworks. Like the milk fritters that follow this recipe, one can buy *fritole* in every *rosticceria* (which is a sort of delicatessen) in Venice. Venetians eat them as snacks at any time of day and evening.

1 oz. dry yeast	*⅓ cup finely chopped*
4 cups flour	*candied fruit*
1½ tbsp. sugar	*1½ cups raisins*
pinch of salt	*2 tbsp. powdered sugar*
⅓ cup pine nuts	

Dissolve yeast in lukewarm water. Add ½ cup flour and 1 tsp. sugar. Let rise for 1½ hours. Sift rest of flour in mixing bowl with salt and rest of sugar; add yeast mixture, pine nuts, fruit, and enough water to make a soft batter. Beat well. Drop one tablespoonful of batter into hot deep fat, and fry until golden. Continue until all the batter is used up. Sprinkle fritters with powdered sugar before serving.

Frittura di Latte alla Bellunese
(MILK FRITTERS BELLUNO STYLE)

1 tbsp. butter
2 tbsp. granulated sugar
2 cups milk
3 eggs

1 tsp. salt
1 tsp. grated lemon rind
½ cup bread crumbs
2 tbsp. powdered sugar

Cream butter and granulated sugar in double boiler; add milk, 2 eggs, salt, and grated lemon rind. Mix well; cook for 20 minutes at low heat, continuing mixing until mixture takes consistency of a thick custard. Pour onto large plate. Let cool and cut into squares or lozenges. Dip into 1 slightly beaten egg and roll in bread crumbs. Fry in shortening and serve sprinkled with powdered sugar.

Gubana (Veneto)
(GUBANA VENETO STYLE)

This is another fruit and nut roll typical of the Veneto region. The dough is even lighter than that used in the *dolce Mirella* (p. 126) and is somewhat similar to the Austrian apple strudel. It is a dessert well suited for afternoon tea or coffee and a buffet party.

Dough:
See recipe for pasta sfoglia,
p. 4.

Filling:

¾ cup bread crumbs	¾ cup chopped walnuts
¾ cup raisins	2 jiggers Grappa (or vodka)
¾ cup pine nuts	½ cup butter

Roll out dough ⅛" thick. Mix bread crumbs, raisins, pine nuts, and walnuts with Grappa and melted butter. Spread mixture on dough and roll up. Seal well at edges and place on greased baking sheet in snail shape. Bake at 325° for 40–45 minutes or until golden brown.

Pan Dolce di Puglia
(SWEET BREAD PUGLIA STYLE)

This loaf cake will keep fresh and moist for as much as a week if wrapped in waxed paper or aluminum foil. Excellent for breakfast and afternoon tea.

2½ cups flour	¾ cup milk
1 tsp. salt	½ cup olive oil
2 tsp. baking powder	1 tbsp. flour
¾ cup sugar	½ cup raisins
2 eggs	grated rind of ½ lemon

Sift flour into a mixing bowl with salt and baking powder. Add sugar, eggs, milk, and oil. Beat well, possibly with electric mixer. Sprinkle 1 tbsp. of flour on a paper towel and roll raisins about in it until they are well coated. Add floured raisins and lemon rind to batter. Pour batter into well-greased and floured rectangular pan 9" × 5", 3" deep. Bake at 325° for 45 minutes.

Panettone di Milano
(PANETTONE MILANESE STYLE)

The making of *panettone* requires so much time and work
that I have given you a recipe that will make two at the same
time. If each *panettone* is well wrapped in aluminum foil, it
will last over a week without losing any of its freshness. But
I guarantee that it will disappear very fast. It can be used
for breakfast, afternoon snacks, coffee or tea, and buffet
parties. It is one of the lightest yeast cakes I know. The
homemade version is dome-shaped, while the commercial
type resembles the Russian *Kulich*—cylindrical around and
puffy and rounded on top. Unlike the *Kulich, panettone's* crisp
and golden brown crust is untouched by any decorations or
icings. Its name, like those of other famous Italian holiday
cakes, comes from *pane*, meaning "bread." Actually, they are
all glorified sweet bread rolls, and the history of their evolu-
tion is told in a poetic 15th-century story in which a certain Ughetto degli Atellani, a Milanese boy of noble family,
fell in love with a baker's beautiful daughter. In order to be
near the girl, Ughetto went to work as an apprentice for the
baker. The competition of a new bakery had made Ughetto's
master lose most of his customers, so, in order to improve the
business, Ughetto began to add first butter, then sugar (paid
for out of his pocket by the sale of some of his falcons) to the
bread, which he still sold at the same price as before. Business picked up and Ughetto added chopped candied fruit and
several dozen eggs and gave the bread the shape of a *pan
grande*, "big round loaf." Soon the fame of Ughetto's bread
spread all over Milan. On Christmas Eve the boy sold his last
falcons and added a few pounds of raisins to his concoction.
His masterpiece was completed and his reputation made, and,
of course, he married the baker's daughter and they lived
happily ever after.

Nowadays *panettone* is produced by such famous pastry and candy manufacturers as Motta and Alemagna in Milan, and Perugina in Perugia, and is shipped by air freight all over the world. The best times to find it in Italian grocery stores are Christmas and Easter. Then you can be sure that it is fresh and you need not go through the process of making it yourself.

A variety of *panettone* is the *pandoro di Verona*, "golden bread of Verona," which is baked in two-quart cake forms and sprinkled with sugar. No candied fruit or raisins are added to the dough, which is very much like that of *panettone*. The Genovese have a *pandolce*, "sweet bread," which they claim is the original version of *panettone*. It is also made with yeast dough, and besides candied fruit and raisins, it has pistachio nuts and fennel seeds.

1½ pkg. dry yeast	*¾ cup raisins*
6 cups flour	*1 tsp. salt*
1¼ cups sugar	*1½ cups butter*
½ cup candied orange and lemon peel	*10 yolks*
	2 whole eggs

Dissolve yeast in a little lukewarm water and set aside for ½ hour. Add 1 cup flour, place on a floured board, and make a very soft dough. Shape into a small ball and put into a bowl. Cover it with a cloth in a warm place and let dough stand for about 3 hours. Turn out on board; add 1 cup sugar and more lukewarm water, and knead well. Return to bowl and let rise for 2 hours. Chop candied fruit; moisten raisins with water. Put rest of flour with salt on board; make a hole in middle and add melted butter, rest of sugar, 10 yolks, 2 whole eggs kept at room temperature, and yeast dough. Mix well and knead for about 20 minutes, until dough is firm and smooth. Add candied fruit and raisins and knead some more. Divide dough into two pieces; shape into two balls. Place on a greased baking sheet; leave in warm place for about 5–6 hours, until double in size. Cut crosses on top and put a little butter on each. Bake at 350° for about 1 hour or until golden brown.

Note: It is advisable to start working on dough in the morning in order to have *panettone* ready by evening.

Panforte di Siena
(PANFORTE SIENA STYLE)

Panforte, like *panettone*, is made commercially and can be found under picturesque wrappers and aluminum foil in Italian grocery stores practically all the year long. Its preparation does not require much time or work, and I prefer to make it myself, especially since this recipe was given to me by a Tuscan pastry chef who boasted that his *panforte* has been a family specialty since the 15th century. It is only about 1½" deep, half chewy and half crunchy, and absolutely delicious. It keeps quite a while if wrapped in aluminum foil.

½ cup blanched almonds
½ cup hazelnuts
1 tbsp. butter
1 cup candied orange peel
¾ cup candied lemon peel

¾ cup flour
1 cup honey
1 cup granulated sugar
1 tbsp. powdered sugar

Toast almonds and hazelnuts slightly in 1 tsp. butter. Cut orange and lemon peels finely. Mix all ingredients together, less honey and sugars. Pour honey into a large pan; add granulated sugar and cook at low heat, continuing mixing until almost at boiling point. Add dry ingredients; stir well and remove from heat. Butter and flour a spring cake pan well and pour in mixture. Bake at 300° for about 35 minutes. Serve cold, sprinkled with powdered sugar.

Parrozzo o Pan Rozzo Abruzzese
(PARROZZO, OR RUSTIC BREAD, ABRUZZI STYLE)

This cake is made commercially in Abruzzi, but I have never been able to find it outside Italy. Even in Italy it is not very common. This particular recipe comes from my father's family. It is very light and quite pretty when cut in wedges, on account of the contrast between the golden dough and the chocolate frosting. Its use is the same as that of *panettone* and all similar dry cakes.

Dough:

5 squares unsweetened chocolate	*1 cup ground hazelnuts or almonds*
¾ cup butter	*¾ cup pastry flour*
¾ cup sugar	*1 tsp. baking powder*
6 egg yolks	

Frosting:

3 tbsp. butter	*1½ cups powdered sugar*
3 squares unsweetened chocolate	*1 tsp. vanilla extract*

Melt chocolate in double boiler and set aside to cool. Cream butter and add sugar; mix well. Add egg yolks and beat well; add melted chocolate, hazelnuts, flour, and baking powder. Pour into a 9″ buttered and floured spring baking pan. Bake at 350° for about 40 minutes.

For frosting, place butter, chocolate, sugar, and vanilla in double boiler and cook until well blended. Pour over cake after it has cooled.

Pasticcini Milanesi
(MILANESE PASTRY)

I highly recommend these *pasticcini*, which are actually raisin muffins, to anyone who wants to make the quickest, most delicious and foolproof kind of pastry to serve for breakfast, coffee, or tea. My dear friend May Amfitheatrof, whose English mother and Russian-Italian husband account for her name and cosmopolitanism, used to make these *pasticcini* from her hometown for our afternoon teas during the time when she lived in Los Angeles. I owe her this recipe, and much more than that.

½ cup butter	2 tsp. baking powder
½ cup sugar	pinch of salt
2 eggs	½ cup raisins
1 cup flour	

Cream butter and sugar; add one egg at a time. Sift flour, baking powder and salt; add to butter and egg mixture. Roll raisins in a little flour and stir them into batter. Grease and flour a muffin pan; place 2 tbsp. mixture in each of a dozen cups. Bake at 350° for 20–25 minutes.

Variation: The dough for *pasticcini* can also be used to make marble cake, doubling the measurements. Add 2 heaping tbsp. cocoa to half the dough. Spoon it into a 9″ greased pan, alternating it with spoonfuls of the other half, and run a knife through to give a marbled effect. The oven temperature is the same as for the pastry, but the time is longer —about 40 minutes.

Ricotta al Caffè Pietrasanta
(COFFEE RICOTTA PIETRASANTA STYLE) *Good* ?

A less traditional version of this dessert features whiskey as a substitute for rum. That's how this dessert was introduced to my husband and me by the great sculptor Henry Moore, who has a summer house in Italy, during the memorable tour we took with him through the marble caves of the mountain Altissimo, near Pietrasanta.

¾ lb. ricotta	6 tsp. powdered instant
¾ cup sugar	coffee
	1 jigger rum

Beat ricotta, sugar, coffee, and rum together until creamy. Place in refrigerator and let stand for at least 1 hour before serving.

Rotolo di Marmellata Gisella (Abruzzi)
(GISELLA'S JAM ROLL ABRUZZI STYLE)

This recipe was given to me by my grandparents' eccentric housekeeper, Gisella. She had gone to live with my grandparents when she was barely 20 and was particularly devoted to my grandfather, whom she followed to Venice, where we were living, after the destruction of his house during the war. It was then that she taught me how to make her one and only specialty. I remember her stressing over and over again how the dough should be still soft and pliable when it was taken out of the oven in order to roll it up properly. And she always took a great pride in the pretty design of the slices, with their concentric bicolored stripes. It is perhaps a little too dry to serve after dinner. It is better suited for an afternoon coffee or tea and excellent for children's snacks.

2 *eggs, separated*   ½ *cup flour*
¼ *cup sugar*   *any fruit preserve*

Beat egg whites stiff; add yolks one by one. Beat well and add sugar. Beat for one more minute; add flour. Pour mixture into 13″ × 9″, 2″ deep baking pan, well buttered and floured. Bake at 325° for about 10 minutes, without letting it dry up. Remove carefully from pan; put on a board, spread with your favorite jam, and roll up. Let cool; slice. Arrange slices in a serving dish.

Rotolo di Ricotta alla Napoletana
 (RICOTTA ROLL NEAPOLITAN STYLE)

This is a typical southern Italian dessert. The use of ricotta, a very light, practically nonfat cheese, is very common in Italy. It is found in a variety of dishes, such as the famous lasagna and a special kind of ravioli, and in salty or sweet fritters. The addition of raisins, pine nuts or almonds, and candied fruit gives an unmistakeably Neapolitan flavor. The filling is basically the same as that of the Sicilian *cannoli* (p. 118). Like the *cannoli*, it is a very tasty and not very delicate dessert better suited to a family Sunday luncheon or supper than a formal dinner. It should be served, like the *cannoli*, with sweet Marsala wine.

Dough:

1 *cup flour*
⅓ *cup sugar*
1 *tsp. baking powder*

2 *eggs*
⅓ *cup milk*

ADDED MORE FLOUR.

Filling: too much for Recipe.

1 *lb. ricotta*
2 *eggs*
½ *cup sugar*
⅓ *cup raisins*

¼ *cup pine nuts or*
chopped almonds
¼ *cup candied fruit*
1 *tsp. rum extract*
1 *egg yolk*

Sift dry ingredients together on a board; add the 2 eggs and milk to make a soft dough. Divide into two rectangular pieces and roll out flat.

Mix all ingredients for filling in a bowl and spread on both pieces of dough. Roll up and brush with egg yolk. Place on greased and floured baking sheet. Bake at 325° for 40 minutes. Serve cool.

Torrone di Cremona
(NOUGAT CANDY CREMONA STYLE)

The *torrone* is a very ancient dessert, probably because its main ingredient is honey, which was the first sweetener ever used. One of its first recipes is found in the Roman Apicius' cookbook and included pepper, whole eggs, and milk, which must have produced a *torrone* somewhat different from the one we know.

It was at the court of the Visconti in Cremona, on the occasion of the wedding banquet for Bianca Maria Visconti and Francesco Sforza, that the *torrone* graced the tables in its final smooth white vest.

The *torrone* is always present in every Italian family at

Christmas and during other festivities, and is served at the end of the dinner with dried and candied fruit and sweet wines such as Moscato d'Asti (natural or sparkling) and Marsala. One variety of *torrone* comes covered with a solid crust of chocolate. Personally, I prefer it without chocolate, which tends to make the delicate taste of honey and almonds disappear. A good *torrone* should be hard, but not too difficult to cut up with a knife. In Italy it is produced commercially by a few reputable manufacturers. I cannot understand, however, why even the best among them export a kind of *torrone* which is so chewy as to give a completely erroneous idea to foreigners of what true *torrone* is like. The recipe is, therefore, for those of you who, not having relatives or friends in Italy to ask that genuine *torrone* be shipped to you, want to taste a *torrone* far superior to the imported one.

1½ cups honey	*1¼ cups sugar*
3 cups blanched almonds	*3 egg whites*
1½ cups hazelnuts	*1 grated lemon rind*

Pour honey into large double boiler and cook for 1½ hours, continuing stirring with a very clean wooden spoon.* Toast almonds and hazelnuts in oven until golden brown. Just before honey is ready (when it becomes hard and brittle if dropped from a teaspoon into cold water), put sugar into a small pan with ½ cup water and cook until slightly bluish. Beat egg whites stiff and add to honey. Mix well for 5–6 minutes; add diluted sugar. Mix again for another 5 minutes; add almonds and hazelnuts and grated lemon rind. Mix well and pour into a Pyrex rectangular pan lined with wafers, rice paper or well-buttered waxed paper. Level mixture with a knife and cover with another sheet of buttered paper. Place a weight on top and set aside for ½ hour. Turn inside down on a board and slice into small rectangular pieces. Keep wrapped in aluminum foil.

* It would be advisable to make this dessert with a friend, so that you can take turns stirring honey.

Torta di Ricotta alla Veneziana
(RICOTTA TART VENETIAN STYLE)

This is my own version. Some measurements can be altered at will—more eggs, sugar, or ricotta added—and the end result is just as good. It is moist, filling but not rich, a simple dessert well suited for snacks or light suppers and welcomed by children and adults alike.

1 tbsp. flour	*1 lb. ricotta*
1 tsp. baking powder	*grated rind of 1 lemon or*
3 tbsp. sugar	*1 orange*
2 eggs, separated	*⅓ cup raisins*

Sift flour and baking powder together; add sugar, egg yolks, ricotta, lemon or orange rind, and raisins which have been rolled in flour. Fold in stiffly beaten egg whites; pour into a 9″ greased and floured baking pan. Bake at 325° for 45 minutes.

Variation: With this recipe one can also make *Frittelle di ricotta* (Ricotta Fritters): Add ½ lb. powdered almond macaroons to the other ingredients, spread dough 1″ thick, cut into diamond shapes; flour them, dip in beaten egg, roll in bread crumbs, and fry in vegetable shortening until golden brown. When cold, sprinkle with powdered sugar.

Torta Reale (Lombardia)
(ROYAL TART LOMBARDY STYLE)

This is a light and dry cake, very easy to make, and excellent with coffee or tea. It can also be used for a birthday cake, with icing and decorations.

½ cup butter	2 cups flour
½ cup sugar	3 tsp. baking powder
3 eggs	¼ tsp. salt
1 tsp. vanilla extract	7½ tbsp. milk

Cream butter with sugar. Add eggs, one by one, and vanilla; beat well. Sift together flour, baking powder, and salt, adding to mixture by tablespoon, alternating with milk. Bake in a greased and floured 9″ pan at 325° for about 45 minutes.

Zelten Trentino
(ZELTEN   TRENTO STYLE)

Many years ago I stopped with some friends in a small hotel on the Alps and I asked if they had something else besides the usual puffed omelette filled with jam which we used to have there. They produced a *zelten* just out of the oven, golden and fragrant. We tasted it and we all loved it —and, of course, I asked for its recipe, which the cook kindly gave me.

1½ pkg. active dry yeast
4 cups flour
pinch salt
1¾ cups milk
½ cup almonds
½ cup walnuts

½ cup dry figs
2 jiggers Kirsch
½ cup raisins
½ cup butter
2 eggs
1 egg yolk

Dissolve yeast in ½ cup lukewarm water; add to half the flour, salt, and ½ cup milk. Make a soft dough, kneading well. Place in a greased bowl; cover with a cloth. Let rise in warm place until double in size (about 1½ hours). Chop almonds—except 6 for decoration—walnuts, and figs and put into a bowl. Pour Kirsch on top and set aside. Put dough on lightly floured board, add rest of flour and milk, knead well and add fruit mixture, raisins, melted butter, and 2 eggs. Knead again and let rise until double. Knead again, shape into an oval, and place on greased baking sheet. Brush with egg yolk and decorate with almond slivers. Let rise again for 30 minutes. Bake at 325° for about 45 minutes.

Index

Index